© 2025 Gelita Mimms
Published by G.Eye.M. LLC
All rights reserved.

No part of this publication may be reproduced, stored in a retrieval system, or transmitted in any form or by any means—electronic, mechanical, photocopying, recording, or otherwise—without the prior written permission of the publisher, except by a reviewer who may quote brief passages for review or educational purposes.

This book is for informational and inspirational purposes only. The author and publisher assume no responsibility for any outcome that may result from the use of the information presented.

ISBN (Print): 978-1-7344156-3-6
Printed in the United States of America.

For bulk orders, speaking engagements, or media inquiries, visit:
www.RaiseYourInnerGEE.com

This book is dedicated to my daughter, Shamiah. Thank you for making sure I never gave up!

Chapter 1: Introduction to Manifestation 1
Chapter 2: The Foundations of Manifestation 4
Chapter 3: Gratitude as the Cornerstone 15
Chapter 4: The Power of Belief 24
Chapter 5: The G.E.E. Framework 30
Chapter 6: Driving Your Dreams into Reality 46
Chapter 7: The Power of Vibration 65
Chapter 8: The Science of Manifestation 71
Chapter 9: Breaking the Chains of Limiting Beliefs 76
Chapter 10: Alignment and Trust in the Universe 83
Chapter 11: Taking Inspired Action 89
Chapter 12: Manifesting Through Action 94
Chapter 13: Visualization Mastery 100
Chapter 14: Manifestation Blocks 106
Chapter 15: The Power of Surrender 110
Chapter 16: Manifesting Through Challenges 116
Chapter 17: Health and Well-Being 122
Chapter 18: Living Like a G.E.E.: Gratitude, Emotion, and Elevation in Action 129

Preface

Manifest Like a G.E.E.

Every journey starts with a spark, and mine lit up over 20 years ago when I first stumbled across the idea of manifestation. The thought that my mind, emotions, and beliefs could shape my reality felt like discovering the universe's best-kept secret. I was all in.

But let me be honest. It wasn't all magic and miracles right away. Like so many others, I tried visualizing, repeating all the affirmations, and wishing on every dream, and still ended up asking myself, What am I missing? Why isn't this working?
It wasn't until years later, through relentless curiosity, personal growth, and sometimes humbling lessons, that I uncovered the truth: Manifestation isn't about wishful thinking. It's about alignment. It's about aligning your energy, actions, and beliefs with your vision. It's about embodying the gratitude, emotion, and elevation that create the conditions for miracles. It's about transforming from the inside out, becoming the version of you that naturally attracts your desires.

Along the way, I experienced incredible highs, like manifesting a car in just 27 days when the odds seemed impossible. But I also faced challenging moments when fear, doubt, and impatience got the best of me. Those experiences taught me the core truths about manifestation and, more importantly, about myself. I learned to trust the process even when nothing seemed to be happening. I learned to quiet the inner critic that whispered, "This doesn't work; you're delusional." And I learned to stay in alignment through every twist and turn.

That's where the G.E.E. Framework comes in: Gratitude, Emotion, and Elevation. G.E.E. isn't just a cute acronym. It's the heartbeat of how I live, coach, and manifest. These three pillars became my compass, helping me shift from confusion to clarity, from wishing to receiving. Gratitude grounds your energy. Emotion amplifies your frequency. Elevation aligns you with your highest self. Throughout this book, you'll see how these three elements work together to create powerful results, not just in theory, but in real life.

Raise Your Inner G.E.E. was born in the middle of a deep season of personal growth. I was in conversation when someone changed the emphasis on the word "energy," and I heard it… Inner GEE. It landed in my spirit like a download. I'm Gee, and I'm focusing on cultivating and raising my inner self, so when I heard 'Inner GEE' it felt like the universe was speaking my name. The vision lit up. The message got louder. The purpose made sense. Gratitude. Emotion. Elevation. I knew this was the key to living in complete alignment and manifesting with power. And I knew I had to share it.

And now, here we are.

Manifest Like a G.E.E. isn't just a book about how to manifest. It's a guide to unlocking the limitless power that already exists within you. Through deeply personal stories, hands-on practices, and insights that bridge science with soul, I'll show you how to transform your mindset, elevate your energy, and align with the life you want to live.

This book is different because it's real. You won't just read about the theory of manifestation, you'll see it in action. You'll witness the ups and downs, the wins and lessons, and the practical steps that create transformation. It's not about magic; it's about mastery of your thoughts, emotions, and beliefs.

Manifestation isn't just about getting what you want; it's about becoming who you want to be. When you embody gratitude, belief, and inspired action, you unlock a vibration that aligns with your highest self. And from that place, there are no limits to what you can achieve.

As you dive into this book, I invite you to approach it with an open heart and mind. Engage with the exercises, reflect on the stories, and most importantly, trust yourself. You're not a passive participant in your story; you're the creator. Your dreams are not just wishes; they're invitations from the universe to rise into your greatness.

Why This Book Is Different

Manifest Like A G.E.E. isn't just another book about the Law of Attraction. What makes this book unique is the combination of practical techniques, universal truths, and deeply personal stories that show you exactly how manifestation works in real life. I'll share examples of my own manifestations, some miraculous, some challenging, but all deeply transformational, to help you see that manifestation isn't just a theory; it's a practice.

Through this book, you'll gain not only the tools but also the mindset needed to transform your life. It's a step-by-step guide to bridging the gap between where you are now and where you want to be. Whether you're manifesting love, abundance, health, or personal growth, this book provides the clarity, strategies, and inspiration to make your dreams a reality. Along the way, you'll discover how to align with your most authentic self and unlock the limitless potential already within you.

You'll learn how to:

- Clarify your desires and set powerful intentions.
- Shift your vibration to align with your goals.
- Overcome limiting beliefs that block your success.
- Take inspired action and trust the process.
- Celebrate every manifestation, big or small, to build momentum.
- Use gratitude as a foundation to amplify manifestation power.
- Master the art of visualization to bring desires to life.
- Navigate challenges and setbacks while maintaining alignment.
- Harness the science of manifestation to reprogram your mind.
- Apply manifestation principles to areas like health, relationships, and well-being.
- Step into your highest self by raising your Inner G.E.E. (Gratitude, Emotion, Elevation).
- Understanding the G.E.E. Framework

- We'll dive deep into the foundations of manifestation, explore the science of vibration and energy, and uncover powerful techniques to raise your vibration and create lasting change. You'll learn how to harness the power of gratitude, belief, and inspired action to manifest everything from financial abundance to fulfilling relationships.

- The journey to your best life begins now.

Are you ready to Manifest Like a G.E.E.?

PART 1: LAYING THE FOUNDATION

Chapter 1: Introduction to Manifestation

Welcome to the beginning of a life-changing journey! By picking up this book, you've taken a bold and empowering step toward transforming your reality and stepping into the role of a deliberate creator. The path ahead will unlock infinite possibilities and help you access the power within you, the power you've always had but may not have fully realized. I'm beyond excited to guide you through this process and help you step into your full potential.

Let's dive right in with a fundamental question: What is manifestation? At its core, to manifest means to bring something into your reality by making it clear or obvious to the mind or eye. Sounds straightforward, right? But let's be real, getting clear about what you genuinely want can sometimes feel like trying to find a single star in a galaxy of possibilities. That's where this book comes in. With practical techniques and proven strategies, you'll be able to get crystal-clear about your desires and deliberately turn your thoughts into things.

Manifestation is much more than wishful thinking; it's about consciously working with the Universal Laws of Attraction and Vibration. These laws govern the energy of the universe and influence how we attract people, circumstances, and experiences into our lives. Whether you realize it or not, you've been manifesting your entire life. The difference now? You're going to learn how to do it deliberately, and Manifest Like a G.E.E. to create a life filled with abundance, love, joy, and purpose. The life you've dreamed of is waiting.

Let's begin.

Manifestation Is Always Happening

You are always manifesting. Every thought, feeling, and belief you hold sends out a vibrational signal to the universe, and the universe responds by bringing you experiences that match that vibration.

Have you noticed that if you stress about being late, the universe suddenly joins in? Your keys pull a disappearing act, traffic turns into a parking lot, and surprise, there's roadwork on your usual shortcut. Boom. You're late. That's manifestation doing its thing. Your focus on being late, coupled with feelings of stress and anxiety, creates a vibration that attracts the very circumstances you were trying to avoid.

Now imagine flipping that script. Instead of focusing on the problem, you focus on the preferred outcome. You imagine yourself arriving on time, feeling calm and collected, and the universe aligns circumstances to make that your reality. The process is the same; it's just a matter of shifting your focus and vibration.

The first step to mastering manifestation is accepting this truth: you are a powerful creator. Your current reality is the result of your past thoughts, feelings, and beliefs. I know. It can be a tough pill to swallow, especially if your reality includes challenges like debt, heartbreak, or health issues. But the good news is that if you created your current reality, you can create a new one.

Manifestation is not about blaming yourself for past struggles. It's about empowering yourself to create a better future. It's about taking responsibility for your energy and using it to design a life that feels aligned with your dreams. Jim Carrey famously wrote himself a ten-million-dollar check for "acting services rendered" long before he was successful. He later received that exact amount for his role in Dumb and Dumber.

Take a moment to let this truth sink in: You are worthy of your dreams. Whatever your heart desires, whether it's love, wealth, health, or peace, is not only possible but already waiting for you. The only thing standing between you and your dreams is your willingness to believe in your power and take the first step.

Manifestation is the art of turning your thoughts into reality, but to truly harness its power, you must understand its underlying principles. It's not just about wishing for what you want; it's about aligning your energy, beliefs, and actions with your desires.

Now that you know the incredible power you hold as a creator, it's time to explore the foundational principles that make manifestation possible. In the next chapter, *The Foundations of Manifestation*, we'll break down the universal laws and practices that turn your desires into tangible realities.

Let's dive deeper into the magic of manifestation and discover the tools that will transform your life and help you *Manifest Like a G.E.E.* every step of the way.

Chapter 2: The Foundations of Manifestation

Manifestation is a process that works whether you believe in it or not. Every thought, feeling, and belief sends out a vibration to the universe, and the universe mirrors it back to you in the form of your experiences. Understanding the foundational principles of manifestation gives you the power to shift from unconsciously to deliberately creating.

At its core, manifestation is about alignment. It's not just about wishing for what you want or visualizing it once and hoping for the best. It's about becoming the energetic match for your desires. When your thoughts, feelings, and beliefs align with what you want, you activate the powerful forces of the universe to bring it into your reality.

The laws of the universe are unbreakable. They're constant, reliable, and always at work, whether you notice them or not. Just like gravity, these laws never take a day off; they're always in motion, always responding to energy, and constantly shaping your reality.

The Law of Vibration: Constant Motion and Vibration

Most people have heard of the Law of Attraction, but many don't realize it works through the Law of Vibration. The Law of Vibration is the foundation. It is the primary law and the energy behind everything that exists. Everything in the universe, including your thoughts, emotions, words, and physical body, vibrates at a particular frequency. Those vibrations send signals into the universe, attracting and creating experiences that match your energetic state. When you feel emotions like joy, love, and gratitude, your frequency rises, and you naturally call in more aligned, uplifting experiences. When fear, doubt, or frustration take over, your frequency lowers, and you begin to create experiences that mirror that same energy.

Think of it like tuning a radio. To hear the station you want, you have to set the dial to precisely the right frequency. If you're even slightly off, the result is static and confusion. Your energy works the same way. The frequency you hold determines the experiences you create. If you want to manifest abundance, for example, you have to tune your vibration to the energy of abundance. You do this by feeling grateful, confident, and open to receiving, even before your reality shows the results.

Tuning to the desired frequency is where alignment comes in. Alignment is what keeps your vibration steady and consistent with what you want to create. It's not just about thinking positive thoughts; it's about matching your energy, emotions, and actions to the frequency of your desires.

When your inner world and your outer actions are in sync, you move in harmony with the energy of what you're calling in, whether it's good or bad, and that's when manifestation becomes effortless.

Alignment is how you stay in harmony with your frequency. Your emotions reveal whether you're tuned in to what you want or tuned in to what you don't want. When you feel joy, gratitude, and excitement, you're in sync with your desires, and life responds with flow, ease, and opportunity. When you fall into fear, doubt, or frustration, your energy shifts, and the outer world reflects that back through resistance or unwanted situations.

Alignment is always visible. It shows up through perfect timing, the right people, and those moments that make you say, "This is meant for me." When things feel off, it's not a punishment. It is feedback, and a sign that your vibration needs a reset, which you can choose to do in an instant. Awareness is your opportunity to recalibrate. Take a breath, center yourself, and shift toward gratitude. Let your emotions lift one step at a time until you feel lighter. The more you practice this, the more naturally you'll recognize when you tune in or out of alignment, and the faster you'll return to the frequency that matches your desires.

The Law of Attraction: Like Attracts Like

The Law of Attraction builds on the Law of Vibration. You attract based on your vibration level. Whatever frequency you hold within yourself will draw in experiences, people, and opportunities that match it. The energy you project through your thoughts, emotions, and beliefs creates a magnetic field that pulls similar vibrations into your experience.

Think of your vibration as the signal and the Law of Attraction as the response. The universe is always listening to the energy you are sending out. It does not respond to words alone; it responds to the emotion and intention behind them. You can say affirmations every day, but if you are still carrying doubt or fear, your signal becomes mixed, and your results will reflect that. Imagine you are trying to manifest love. If your thoughts are of self-doubt or fear of rejection, and your feelings reflect loneliness or unworthiness, you are vibrating at a frequency that attracts more of the same. The relationships that appear will often feel unfulfilling or unavailable. When you shift your focus toward self-love, gratitude for the love already present in your life, and the joy of connection, you begin to align with the energy of love itself. The shift always happens on the inside before it shows up on the outside.

The key is to focus not on what you lack but on what you already have and what you desire to feel. The focus is not about ignoring your reality; it is about learning to guide your energy toward the reality you want to experience. When you think, feel, and act as if your desire is already present, you activate the frequency that draws it closer.

The Law of Attraction is not a trick or a shortcut. It is a mirror that reflects the vibration you hold most consistently. When you nurture emotions like gratitude, joy, and trust, you naturally attract more experiences that carry those same vibrations. As your inner energy rises, your outer world rearranges itself to match it.

The Law of Circulation: Abundance in Motion

While the Law of Attraction explains how we attract experiences, the Law of Circulation reminds us that energy, money, love, and opportunity all flow in cycles. Abundance is not meant to sit still. It's intended to move. It must be shared, given, and released to remain alive in your life.

Circulation is the energetic rhythm of prosperity. Just as blood flows through the body or currency circulates in the economy, energy must move freely to remain vibrant. When we give from a space of trust and intention, not fear or obligation, we tell the Universe: *I believe in your infinite supply. I'm not clinging. I'm co-creating.* And in doing so, we open the channel for more to move toward us.

This doesn't just apply to money. Giving your time, support, ideas, compliments, knowledge, forgiveness, or simply clearing space in your environment; all of it is circulation. Whether you're donating clothes, paying a bill with gratitude, releasing a grudge, or uplifting someone's spirit, you're signaling that you're available for more.

You're showing the Universe that you trust the flow.

Have you ever cleaned out your closet and suddenly received new clothes? Or given your last few dollars only to be surprised by a refund, gift, or new client? That's circulation in action. It doesn't always return from the same source, or in the same form, but it always returns, often multiplied and always right on time.

The problem is, many people try to manifest while holding on tightly, gripping resources, withholding love, and guarding time as if it's running out. But hoarding blocks the flow. Stagnation breeds scarcity. Circulation invites miracles.

You must exhale to inhale. You must let go to receive. This is the dance of co-creation.

So the next time you're waiting on a financial breakthrough, clarity, or a significant opportunity, ask yourself: *What can I release right now with faith? What can I circulate?* That act of letting go might be the key to your next manifestation.

When you align with the Law of Circulation, you become more than a collector of blessings; you become a vessel. A steward. A channel. And through you, abundance doesn't just visit... it flows.

Manifestation Across Dimensions: Gratitude, Emotion, and Elevation

We live in a multi-dimensional universe, and your ability to Manifest Like a G.E.E. correlates to the level of consciousness you are operating from. Every dimension carries a unique vibration and a different way of perceiving and creating reality. There are many dimensions of existence. However, three key ones, 3D, 4D, and 5D, play a powerful role in how your manifestations unfold and tie directly into the G.E.E. framework of gratitude, emotion, and elevation.

Each dimension reflects your awareness, your beliefs, and the energy you hold. The more you expand your consciousness, the more fluid and effortless manifestation becomes. As you raise your vibration, you move from reacting to your circumstances to consciously shaping them. You begin to see that you are not just existing in these dimensions; you are moving between them all the time through your thoughts, emotions, and focus.

Understanding the 3D, 4D, and 5D is not about escaping the human experience. It is about learning how energy flows through these layers so you can create with greater intention and ease. Think of them as stages of energetic awareness, each one offering a new level of clarity, power, and alignment. The more you align with higher frequencies, the more you experience synchronicities, divine timing, and manifestations that feel guided rather than forced.

Let's explore how each dimension influences the way you manifest and how you can move fluidly between them.

3D: The Physical Dimension: Reality, Consciousness, and Gratitude

The third dimension, or 3D, is the physical world you can see, touch, and measure. It is the dimension of conscious awareness and tangible experience. In 3D, life appears solid and predictable, and it often feels like cause and effect are the only rules. The 3D is also where the problems exist. You see challenges, limitations, and obstacles that seem real and unavoidable because this dimension relies on physical evidence and logic.

The 3D world is not your enemy; it is your classroom. It reveals what you still believe about yourself and what vibrations you are sending out. Gratitude is the key here. When you practice gratitude even in the middle of difficulty, you begin to shift your energy. Gratitude moves you from focusing on what is wrong to recognizing what is working. It softens resistance and opens the door to new possibilities.

4D: The Mental Dimension: Imagination, Subconscious, and Emotion

The fourth dimension, or 4D, is the bridge between the physical and spiritual planes. 4D is the realm of thought, imagination, and emotion. It connects your conscious mind to your subconscious patterns. In 4D, you begin to create new energetic blueprints for your reality. The fourth dimension is where the solutions exist. Everything you want to experience first takes shape here, in the form of an idea, a feeling, or an inner vision.

Your imagination in 4D is not fantasy; it is creative energy in motion. The thoughts you think and the emotions you feel here set the frequency for what will manifest later in 3D. Emotion is your power tool in this space. When you feel gratitude, love, and joy as if your desire is already here, you send a clear signal to the universe. The 4D realm teaches you that your feelings create momentum long before anything becomes visible.

5D: The Spiritual Dimension: Meditation, Superconsciousness, and Elevation

The fifth dimension, or 5D, is the space of pure alignment and expanded awareness. In this dimension, you move beyond logic and step into unity with everything around you. The sense of separation fades, and you begin to experience life as energy flowing through and around you. 5D is the realm of the superconscious, where intuition becomes your compass and love becomes your natural state.

Meditation is the gateway into 5D consciousness. Stillness allows you to rise above the noise of daily life and connect with the higher frequency of your true self. Here, manifestation happens through alignment rather than effort. You do not have to push or force outcomes. Instead, you allow them to unfold because your energy is already in harmony with what you desire.

Elevation in this dimension is not about escaping the human experience; it is about expanding it. You see challenges from a higher perspective and respond with peace instead of panic. The more often you enter this elevated state, the more your life reflects flow, clarity, and divine timing. In 5D, you become a conscious co-creator with the universe, and everything you attract carries the frequency of love and harmony.

Manifestation Across All Dimensions
Manifestation is not confined to a single dimension. It is a continuous flow of energy moving through all levels of awareness. Each dimension plays a specific role in the creation process, and together, they form a complete cycle of thought, feeling, and alignment.
- **3D: Identify.** This is where you become aware of what you want by observing your current reality. The contrast and challenges you face reveal your desires and help you clarify your next steps. Gratitude keeps your energy open here, reminding you that every experience is guiding you toward greater alignment.
- **4D: Imagine.** Imagination is where you shift into creation. Through imagination, visualization, and emotion, you align

your energy with the frequency of what you desire. The subconscious begins to accept this new reality as possible. As you feel the joy, gratitude, and excitement of already having it, you start to reprogram your vibration to match your desired outcome.
- **5D: Align.** 5D is where you let go and let the universe co-create with you. Through meditation, presence, and trust, you connect with your higher consciousness and follow inspired action. In this space, you do not chase; you attract. You move with confidence, knowing the energy is already working in your favor.

All three dimensions are essential. You live in 3D, create through 4D, and receive in 5D. The key is to move fluidly between them instead of getting stuck in one. When you learn to identify, imagine, and align with intention, manifestation becomes a natural expression of your energy.

For example, if you are manifesting financial abundance:
- In 3D, you recognize areas of struggle or limitation and set a clear intention for prosperity.
- In 4D, you visualize yourself living in abundance and feel the joy of financial freedom.
- In 5D, you meditate, trust the process, and follow intuitive nudges that guide you toward inspired opportunities.

Each layer supports the next. The physical reveals the desire, the mental creates the vibration, and the spiritual aligns the outcome. Together, the individual layers form a cycle of creation that reflects the flow of the universe itself.

Understanding the foundational principles of manifestation and the dimensions of consciousness allows you to take full ownership of your life. You are the bridge between worlds, the connector between the 3D physical reality, the 4D creative realm, and the 5D flow of higher awareness. Through you, energy becomes experience and thought becomes form.

Every thought you think, every feeling you nurture, and every belief you hold adds a new brushstroke to the masterpiece that is your reality. The more intentionally you align your vibration, the more gracefully your desires flow into your life. Think of each brushstroke as the power of conscious creation. You are both the artist and the art, shaping your world through the energy you embody.

As you move through this journey, remember that manifestation is not a single moment. It is a way of being, rooted in awareness, gratitude, and trust. The process is not about perfection. It is about presence. Celebrate your growth, honor your lessons, and keep returning to alignment. Each step brings you closer to the life your soul already knows is possible.

Building on Gratitude

The foundations of manifestation consist of a combination of your thoughts, emotions, and actions. When these three elements move in harmony, you create a robust, energetic base that supports everything you desire to attract. Alignment allows energy to flow freely, guiding you toward experiences that reflect your highest intentions.

At the center of this process lives one transformative force: gratitude. Gratitude is more than a feeling; it is a vibration that amplifies creation itself. When you focus on what you already appreciate, your energy rises and your perspective expands. You begin to see abundance in every moment, and that awareness calls in even more to be grateful for.

In the next chapter, Gratitude as the Cornerstone, we will explore why gratitude is the ultimate manifestation tool. You will discover how it anchors your energy, strengthens your alignment, and becomes the foundation for a life filled with joy, fulfillment, and limitless possibility.

Chapter 3: Gratitude as the Cornerstone

Gratitude is the foundation of transformation. It is not merely a polite gesture or fleeting feeling. It's a way of being that aligns you with the vibration of abundance, joy, and infinite possibilities. Gratitude opens your heart, shifts your focus, and raises your vibration, making it the ultimate tool for deliberate creation. It isn't just a feeling; it's a state of being. When you're in a state of gratitude, you align yourself with the highest frequencies of joy, abundance, and love. The energy you emit determines what you attract into your life.

It's like when you spill coffee on your shirt, and suddenly, it feels like the whole day spirals downward. But the opposite is also true, and the choice is yours. When you choose to focus on what's going right, even in small ways, your day gets better and better, which isn't a coincidence; it's the power of gratitude. It shifts your focus from lack to abundance, from problems to possibilities, and from frustration to peace. Gratitude teaches you to see the blessings in every moment, even when life isn't perfect. It's not about ignoring challenges but about finding the good amidst them. This shift in perspective changes everything.

Gratitude isn't just about noticing the good stuff. It's about recognizing the beauty, lessons, and blessings in every moment, even the ones that test you. That's where the real power lies. What you focus on will always grow. When you spend your energy thinking about what's missing or what's not working, you're sending a signal that says, "This is my reality." The universe listens and gives you more of the same.

But when you start appreciating what's already good, the small wins, the quiet moments, the simple things, you shift your energy. You tell the universe, "I'm ready for more of this."

Gratitude becomes the bridge between where you are and where you want to be. It turns your focus from lack to abundance and reminds you that there's always something to appreciate, even now. Every time you pause to give thanks, you raise your vibration and open the door to even more blessings. Everything is energy, including your thoughts and emotions. Every time you focus on something, you are sending out a vibration that the universe responds to. Gratitude raises that vibration. It shifts your inner state from resistance to receptivity, from fear to faith, and from scarcity to abundance.

When you practice gratitude, you are not just thinking positive thoughts. You are aligning your energy with the frequency of appreciation. That frequency is magnetic. It draws in more experiences that match the energy of joy, peace, and fulfillment. The more often you hold that vibration, the more your outer world begins to mirror it. Oprah Winfrey frequently says that gratitude was the turning point that shifted her from struggle to abundance.

Gratitude also reprograms your energetic pattern. It softens old habits of worry or lack and teaches your mind and body to expect good things. You begin to feel safe receiving, comfortable expanding, and open to the flow of abundance. Over time, gratitude becomes your natural frequency, and manifestation starts to feel effortless because you are in alignment with what you want.

Have you ever been around someone who radiates positivity even when life is not perfect? Their energy feels light, warm, and contagious. That is the power of gratitude in motion. People who live in a state of appreciation carry a higher vibration, and that frequency naturally draws in joy, love, and opportunity.

Gratitude is magnetic. It shifts your energy from wanting to allowing, from effort to ease. The more you practice it, the more others can feel it around you. Your presence becomes a reminder that peace and abundance are available in every moment. When you live with gratitude as your foundation, you do not have to chase blessings; they will begin to chase you.

Gratitude Across Dimensions:

Gratitude moves with you through every level of awareness. It's the energy that connects your physical world, your imagination, and your higher consciousness. The more you understand how gratitude works across each dimension, the easier it becomes to shift your energy and manifest with flow.

In 3D, gratitude keeps you grounded. 3D is where you focus on the tangible things like your health, your home, your relationships, the blessings you can touch and see. Even when things feel heavy or uncertain, choosing to notice what's good right now shifts your energy instantly. Being grateful for a meal, a hug, or the air you breathe roots you in the present moment, which is where gratitude begins.

In 4D, gratitude becomes a creative force. 4D is where emotion and imagination work together. You start to give thanks for what hasn't shown up yet. You're grateful for the opportunities, relationships, and experiences already forming behind the scenes. When you visualize what you want and feel gratitude as if it's already yours, you're sending a clear message to the universe that you're ready to receive. Emotion is the fuel here. Gratitude in the 4D turns your imagination into a powerful magnet for manifestation.

In 5D, gratitude becomes peace. It's not about asking for anything or waiting for something to happen. It's about trusting that everything is already working in your favor. You give thanks simply for being; for the love, the lessons, the divine timing of it all. In this space, you're not trying to control life. You're flowing with it, so your energy rises and alignment feels natural. Gratitude in the 5D is pure elevation.

When you understand gratitude across these dimensions, you see how it evolves with you. It starts in the physical, expands through emotion, and rises into alignment with something greater. Gratitude isn't just a practice. Gratitude is a way of living that connects you to every level of creation.

Now that you know how gratitude flows through each dimension, let's talk about how to bring it into your everyday life. You move through these layers all the time, through your thoughts, your emotions, and your energy, and each one gives you a chance to shift into a higher vibration.

3D Gratitude: Start with what's real

Take a moment to look around you. What can you appreciate right now? Maybe it's your morning coffee, your body that keeps showing up for you, or the roof over your head. Gratitude starts in the physical world, right where you are. When you take time to notice what's already good, your energy shifts immediately. You begin to see that even when things aren't perfect, there's always something working in your favor.

4D Gratitude: Feel it before you see it

Now move into your imagination. Close your eyes and think about what you're calling in: the relationship, the opportunity, the peace, the abundance. Feel gratitude for it, as if it's already part of your life. Let that feeling build inside you until it feels real. That emotion is what sends the signal out to the universe. The more you practice feeling grateful for what's on its way, the faster it finds you.

5D Gratitude: Surrender and Trust
Finally, take it higher. Please stop trying to control how things unfold and trust that everything is aligning exactly as it should. Take a deep breath and give thanks for the bigger picture, for being guided, protected, and connected to something greater than yourself. In this space, gratitude feels calm and complete. You don't have to chase; you allow.

When you practice gratitude in all three dimensions, you stay in the flow of creation. You learn to appreciate what you have, feel grateful for what's becoming, and trust what you can't yet see. That's the sweet spot, when gratitude becomes your lifestyle.

The Science of Gratitude: Rewiring Your Brain for Joy
Gratitude isn't just a spiritual practice; it's also deeply biological. Every time you express genuine gratitude, your brain releases feel-good chemicals like dopamine and serotonin. These are the chemicals that boost happiness, reduce stress, and create an overall sense of well-being. You're not only feeling better in the moment, but you're also literally training your brain to look for more of what's good.

Science backs this up. Dr. Robert Emmons, one of the leading researchers on gratitude, found that people who practice it regularly experience powerful shifts in their overall health and mindset. They sleep better, have lower blood pressure, and tend to handle stress more gracefully. Gratitude strengthens emotional resilience, improves relationships, and even helps you recover from challenges faster because your brain becomes wired to notice possibilities instead of problems. Think of gratitude as mental fitness. Every time you practice it, you strengthen the neural pathways that focus on positivity. The more you do it, the easier it becomes to see the good, even in difficult situations. Over time, this creates a ripple effect throughout your life. You begin to expect good things, attract better experiences, and feel more at peace within yourself.

Gratitude doesn't ignore reality; it reshapes how you see it. It's the shift that turns ordinary moments into reminders of how supported you genuinely are. The more you practice it, the more your brain learns that joy is your natural state.

Gratitude is often called the secret ingredient in manifestation, and for good reason. It acts as a multiplier, amplifying the energy of your desires and aligning you with the frequency of abundance.

Here's how it works:

1. Gratitude Shifts Your Energy: Feeling grateful instantly raises your vibration.

2. Gratitude Aligns You with Your Desires: When you're grateful for what you have and what's coming, you emit a signal that says, "I trust the universe."

3. Gratitude Keeps You in the Present Moment: Manifestation happens in the now. Gratitude anchors you in the present, where you can fully feel the energy of having your desires.

Simple Gratitude Practices to Raise Your Vibration

Here are some simple, daily practices to help you stay connected to gratitude in every dimension: body, mind, and spirit.

The more you make them part of your routine, the more naturally gratitude becomes your default energy.

Start and End Your Day with Gratitude

Before your feet hit the floor in the morning, take a moment to think of three things you're grateful for. It can be as simple as waking up rested, having clean water, or knowing a new day is full of possibilities. Feel that appreciation for a few quiet seconds and let it set the tone for your day. Before bed, do the same. Reflect on three things that went right, no matter how small. This bookend of gratitude keeps your energy clear and centered from sunrise to sunset.

Gratitude Journaling

Writing down your gratitude takes it deeper. List three to five things you're grateful for each day and be specific. Instead of writing "I'm grateful for my job," try "I'm grateful for the conversation I had with my coworker that made me laugh today." Specificity brings emotion, and emotion strengthens the vibration. Over time, you'll start to notice how many beautiful moments fill your days. Some of which might have gone unnoticed before.

Gratitude Walks

Take a walk and let gratitude guide your awareness. Notice the warmth of the sun, the rhythm of your breath, the color of the sky, or the simple fact that your body allows you to move through the world. With each step, say "thank you" silently or aloud. Gratitude walks are grounding, healing, and powerful reminders that abundance exists all around you when you choose to see it.

Express Gratitude to Others

Don't just feel gratitude, share it. Tell someone why you appreciate them, how they've helped you, or what you admire about them. A quick text, a handwritten note, or a heartfelt conversation can instantly shift both of your energies. When you speak gratitude into someone else's life, it multiplies. The more you express it, the stronger the connection becomes, both with others and with yourself.

Gratitude is an essential building block of manifestation. It shifts your focus, raises your vibration, and aligns you with the energy of abundance. It's the bridge between your current reality and the life you dream of living. By making gratitude a daily practice, you'll find that the universe responds in kind, showering you with blessings, opportunities, and joy. Gratitude is more than a practice; it's a way of life, and it has the power to transform not just your manifestations but your entire reality.

Let gratitude be your superpower. The more you appreciate what you have, the more life gives you to be grateful for. The journey starts with a simple phrase: "Thank you." Gratitude is more than just an emotion; it's the foundation upon which all successful manifestations exist. By cultivating gratitude, you align yourself with the highest frequencies of abundance and joy, creating the perfect conditions for your desires to flow into your life.

But gratitude alone is not enough. To fully harness the power of manifestation, you must also believe, truly and deeply, that your dreams are possible. Jim Carrey, Oprah, and countless others are proof that when you combine gratitude with belief, life rises to meet your energy. Gratitude plants the seeds, but belief is the fertile soil that allows those seeds to grow. It's the invisible force that shapes your reality, transforming thoughts into things and desires into experiences. In the next chapter, we'll explore the power of belief and why it's the most critical component of deliberate creation. You'll learn how to identify limiting beliefs, rewrite them, and cultivate the unshakable confidence needed to manifest your deepest desires.

Let's dive into the transformative power of belief.

Chapter 4: The Power of Belief

Belief is the foundation of manifestation. It's the invisible force that shapes your decisions, actions, and ultimately your reality. What you believe about yourself, others, and the world determines what you experience. When you believe in your dreams with unwavering confidence, you unlock a wellspring of potential. On the flip side, when your beliefs are rooted in doubt or fear, you unconsciously create barriers that keep you from achieving your goals.

Your beliefs act as the blueprint for your life. They influence every thought you think, every feeling you experience, and every action you take. Simply put, you don't attract what you want; you attract what you believe.

Imagine your mind as a fertile garden. Your beliefs are the seeds you plant. If you sow seeds of abundance, worthiness, and possibility, you'll grow a garden full of thriving opportunities. But if you plant seeds of fear, doubt, and scarcity, your garden will reflect those limitations. The challenge is that many of your beliefs are unconscious, shaped by childhood experiences, societal expectations, and past failures. These beliefs often operate in the background, influencing your decisions without your awareness.

The good news? Even if you don't yet realize a belief exists, you have the power to change it. Belief is not only the starting point but also the sustaining force behind manifestation. It's the thread that weaves your intentions into reality, and when cultivated with care, it becomes your most valuable asset in creating a life you love.

Belief serves as the bridge between your desires and your

reality. It's not enough to visualize your goals or repeat affirmations; you must genuinely believe they are possible for you. When you believe in your desires wholeheartedly, you send a clear, consistent signal to the universe, align your energy with the frequency of your goals, and take inspired action without hesitation or doubt. But if your beliefs contradict your desires, you create resistance. For example, if you want to attract wealth but believe "money is the root of all evil," your subconscious will block opportunities for financial abundance.

True belief is not just a fleeting hope or wish; it's a deep, unshakable knowing that what you desire is not only possible but already on its way to you. This belief creates an energetic alignment that allows the universe to work in your favor.

The Science of Belief: Reprogramming Your Mind

Your beliefs are not fixed; they are conditioned patterns that can be reshaped. Neuroscience shows that the brain is constantly changing through neuroplasticity. Dr. Joe Dispenza's research supports this idea, demonstrating how focused thought and elevated emotion can create new neural connections and dissolve old, limiting ones. When you practice new emotional states, you literally teach your brain and body to expect a new reality.

Here's how it works:
- When you think a thought repeatedly, it becomes a belief.
- That belief influences your actions and creates experiences that reinforce the belief.
- The cycle continues, making the belief feel like an unchangeable truth.

For example, if you believe "I'm not good enough," you'll hesitate to pursue opportunities, which leads to missed chances and feelings of failure, reinforcing the belief and creating a self-fulfilling prophecy.

The key to breaking this cycle is to introduce new, empowering beliefs. By consistently focusing on positive thoughts, you can rewire your brain to support your goals.
Limiting beliefs are like invisible walls that keep you stuck. They often masquerade as "facts" or "truths" about your life, but they are simply stories you've accepted as reality.

Common Limiting Beliefs
- "I'm not smart enough to succeed."
- "I don't deserve love."
- "I have to work hard for money."
- "Good things never happen to me."

Practical Exercise: Unearthing Your Beliefs

1. Choose a specific area of your life where you feel stuck (e.g., career, relationships, health).
2. Write down everything you believe about that area. Don't filter yourself, be honest.
3. Look for recurring themes or negative patterns. These are your limiting beliefs.

For example, if your list includes statements like "I'll never get promoted" or "I'm just not leadership material," you've uncovered beliefs that may be blocking your career growth.

Acknowledging these beliefs is not about judgment; it's about awareness. Once you recognize them, you can take the steps needed to replace them with empowering truths.

How to Rewrite Your Beliefs

Rewriting your beliefs requires intention and repetition. It's not about suppressing negative thoughts but replacing them with empowering ones.

Steps to Rewriting Beliefs
1. Acknowledge the Belief: Say it out loud or write it down. For example, "I believe I'm not worthy of success."
2. Challenge the Belief: Ask yourself, "Is this belief absolutely true? What evidence do I have to support it? What evidence contradicts it?"
3. Replace the Belief: Create a new belief that aligns with your desires, such as "I am worthy of success, and I achieve my goals with ease."
4. Reinforce the New Belief: Repeat it daily, visualize it as true, and look for evidence in your life that supports it.

Example in Action:
If you've been told, "You're not good with money," challenge that belief by listing times when you made wise financial decisions. Replace it with, "I manage my money wisely and attract financial abundance."

Rewriting beliefs is a journey, not a one-time event. With each repetition, you create stronger neural connections, making the new belief feel natural and authentic.

Lisa Nichols once believed she was only capable of living a small, limited life, until a powerful moment at her grandmother's funeral inspired her to rewrite that belief and commit to living fully and unapologetically. That decision became the catalyst for transforming her mindset, her mission, and her legacy.

Personal Story: The Raffle Ticket Manifestation

Belief has played a significant role in many of my manifestations, but one particular experience stands out as a profound lesson about the power and limitations of belief.

I attended a networking event that included a raffle for "starving artists." Each participant could purchase tickets, and the cash collected from the ticket sales went into a large jar. Three tickets are being drawn, and the winners will have 1 minute each to perform for the audience. The crowd would vote for the best performer, and the winner would receive the money in the jar.

I bought five tickets and felt an immediate sense of panic. As soon as I had the tickets in my hand, I knew my ticket would be selected. I could feel it in every fiber of my being, but I am not prepared to perform. I had recently written a spoken-word piece, but I wasn't confident I had memorized it.

My friends arrived, and I nervously told them, "They're going to call my number, and I don't know what to do!" One friend offered to perform in my place if I won. They called the first number, which wasn't mine. The second number wasn't mine either. But then, they called my number!

I handed my ticket to my friend, and he performed his rap song. He didn't win, but as I watched the other two performers, I realized something: if I had gone up there, I would have undoubtedly won. I had believed so strongly in the drawing of my ticket, but I didn't believe in my ability to perform. My lack of preparation and confidence cost me a jar filled with over $300.

That experience taught me an invaluable lesson: belief is not just about expecting a result, it's about preparing to receive it. Now, whenever I enter a raffle, I not only believe I'll win, but I make sure I'm ready to claim my prize.

Belief is the bedrock of manifestation, the invisible force that shapes your reality. When you align your thoughts, emotions, and actions with unwavering belief, you activate the universe's limitless potential to work in your favor. But belief is more than just a mental exercise; it requires trust, persistence, and an openness to the unexpected.

And that's exactly where the G.E.E. Framework comes in. In the next chapter, we'll explore how Gratitude, Emotion, and Elevation work together to strengthen your belief, raise your vibration, and align your inner world with the life you're ready to create.

Chapter 5: The G.E.E. Framework

Manifestation is not just about thinking positively or wishing for change. It's about intentionally aligning your thoughts, emotions, and actions with the energy of your desires. That's where the G.E.E. Framework comes in. G.E.E. stands for Gratitude, Emotion, and Elevation. It's a three-part energetic framework I created that has helped me manifest everything from unexpected money to a new car, all by tuning into higher frequencies and becoming a match for what I desire.

This framework is the foundation of how I live, how I manifest, and how I teach others to create change in their lives. Let's break it down.

Gratitude

Gratitude is the anchor. It is the grounding force that brings you back to center and aligns you with abundance. When you practice gratitude deeply and sincerely, you're not just saying thank you. You're saying, "I recognize the good that already exists in my life." That moment of recognition instantly shifts your focus, energy, and vibration. It reminds your mind of what is true and reminds your spirit of what is possible.

But gratitude becomes truly powerful when you start using it as a tool, not just a reaction. Most people express gratitude only when something good happens. You are learning to express gratitude *because* it aligns your energy with the life you want to create. It becomes an intentional practice rather than a momentary feeling. Gratitude is also not limited to what is comfortable. If you only give thanks for what feels good, you miss the deeper transformation that gratitude can bring. Being grateful for your challenges is next-level energy. It requires you to look at what tests you, irritates you, or scares you, and see the growth inside of it. When you can honestly say, "Thank you for this obstacle because it is shaping me into a stronger version of myself," you elevate your vibration in a way few practices can match.

This doesn't mean pretending everything is perfect. It means trusting that everything has purpose. Gratitude becomes a bridge between what is and what can be. It helps you hold both truth and possibility simultaneously. You can acknowledge the challenge and still choose appreciation. That choice shifts your emotional direction and opens you to guidance, clarity, and solutions that you couldn't see before.

To deepen your gratitude practice, I want you to start paying attention to the things you usually overlook. Small wins. Tiny moments. Fleeting blessings. The way a certain song lifts your spirit. The softness of your pillow. Hot water. Clean clothes. A peaceful car ride. Someone holding the door open for you. These seemingly small things carry powerful energy when noticed deliberately. Gratitude grows wherever you place your attention, and when you train your mind to see the good, you begin attracting even more of it.

And if you want to supercharge your manifestations, start giving thanks in advance. Gratitude for the things that haven't shown up yet is one of the strongest signals you can send to the Universe. When you say, "Thank you for my new home," or "Thank you for the opportunities flowing to me," or "Thank you for the peace, love, and wealth already forming in my life," you are speaking from belief. You are speaking from alignment. You are declaring, "I trust that it is already mine."

This type of gratitude shifts you into the energetic frequency of receiving. It prepares your mind to expect what you desire and prepares your spirit to recognize it when it appears. Gratitude in advance turns your manifestation from a hope into an inner knowing.

The Gratitude Practice

Gratitude is the foundation of the G.E.E. Framework because it shifts your energy instantly. When you practice gratitude intentionally, you are training your mind to look for abundance, align with good, and recognize guidance. Gratitude prepares your heart to receive. This practice helps you deepen appreciation for what is already present while opening your energy to what is becoming.

Present-Moment Gratitude
Begin by writing two to three things you are genuinely grateful for right now. These can be simple or profound. Allow yourself to feel the appreciation as you write. Gratitude is a vibration, and your energy responds the moment you lean into it.

Gratitude for What You Are Calling In
Next, write two to three things you are manifesting in the present tense, as if they already exist. This is not pretending. This is alignment. Present-tense gratitude strengthens your belief system and sends a clear signal to the Universe that you are ready to receive.

Examples:
"I am so grateful for the financial stability flowing into my life every week."
"I am grateful for the peaceful mornings in my beautiful new home."
"I am thankful for the consistent clients who love working with me."

Gratitude Scripting

Scripting is gratitude expanded into a story. Instead of writing a list, you write as if you are living the reality you are calling in. This activates your imagination, engages your senses, and brings your future into your present moment.

Examples:

"I am so grateful that I only fly first class now that I am an in-demand speaker. It feels amazing to be invited to events where my flight is covered and I get to travel in comfort and luxury. I love boarding early, settling into my spacious seat, and knowing this is my new normal."

"I am so grateful for the steady stream of opportunities that flow to me. People reach out because they feel connected to my message, and I am honored to speak, serve, and inspire."

"I am grateful that my home feels peaceful, abundant, and aligned. I wake up every morning with sunlight pouring in, and I'm thankful for the blessings that surround me."

Your scripting can be a paragraph, a few sentences, or a full page. What matters is that the emotion is real.

When Gratitude Feels Hard

There will be days when gratitude feels difficult. On those days, focus on the smallest good you can find. Be grateful for the lesson, not the discomfort. Use the prompt: "What is this situation strengthening in me?" Gratitude during challenging moments elevates your vibration quickly and shifts you into alignment.

The Gratitude Flow

To bring this practice together, follow this simple sequence:
- Write two to three things you are grateful for now.

- Write two to three things you are grateful for that you are calling in. Write them in the present tense.
- Script one gratitude-based scene from your future.
- Take a deep breath and let the emotion of gratitude settle in your body.
-

Practicing gratitude in this intentional way prepares your energy for manifestation and aligns you with the version of yourself who is ready to receive.

Emotion

Emotion is your energetic signature. It is how the Universe reads you and understands what you are available for. Every thought you think carries a frequency, but it is your emotions that determine how loudly that frequency is broadcast. You can think a hundred positive thoughts, but if you are feeling doubt, fear, or unworthiness underneath those thoughts, that emotion becomes the true signal you are sending out.

Learning how to feel on purpose is a game-changer. Most people wait for something outside of them to happen so they can feel good. They wait for the promotion to feel proud, the relationship to feel loved, and the money to feel secure. But manifestation works in the opposite direction. You feel the emotion first. You choose it intentionally. You decide to feel calm, confident, abundant, or worthy before anything shifts on the outside. When you align with the emotion of your desire before it manifests, you collapse the timeline. You call it in faster because you are becoming the vibrational match to it now, not someday.

Your emotions are also powerful indicators. When you feel good, you are in alignment with your higher self. You are connected to the truth of who you are and what is possible for you. When you feel bad, it is not a punishment or a sign of failure. It is simply feedback.

It is your inner guidance saying, "The way you are thinking about this right now is not aligned with the truth of who you are." This is why emotions matter. They help you course-correct quickly instead of spiraling deeper into fear or doubt. Use them as a compass. They will always show you what needs to shift.

Another key piece is understanding that emotions do not just happen to you. They are responses to the thoughts you choose to focus on. When you shift your focus, you shift your emotion. This does not mean you ignore what you feel. It means learning to guide your feelings rather than being controlled by them. Allow yourself to feel what comes up, acknowledge it, and then choose a thought that feels a little better. Emotional mastery is a series of gentle shifts, not giant leaps.

Visualization and imagination are powerful tools in this process because your body responds to them as if they are real. When you close your eyes and imagine the leather seats of the car you want, hear the laughter filling the room at your dream celebration, or taste the meal you are preparing in your beautiful new kitchen, your nervous system does not know the difference between an imagined experience and a physical one. When you emotionally experience your manifestation before it arrives, you begin calling it closer and closer. You become the version of yourself who already has it, and the Universe responds to that version of you.

This is why emotion is such an essential part of manifestation. It is not about pretending or forcing positivity. It is about aligning your inner state with the reality you want to create. The more consistently you feel the emotions connected to your desire, the more naturally your outer world begins to rearrange itself to match them.

The Emotion Practice

Emotion is the vibrational language of manifestation. It is how your energy communicates with the Universe and how your inner world shapes your outer world. When you learn to feel on purpose instead of waiting for life to give you permission, you step into your power as a creator.

This practice helps you align with your emotions so you can embody the feelings that match the reality you want to manifest.

Emotional Visualization

Choose one desire and visualize yourself already living it. Instead of viewing the scene from a distance, step inside it. Engage all your senses so your body responds as if the moment were happening now.

Ask yourself:
What do I see?
What do I hear?
What do I feel against my skin?
What scents are in the air?
What am I tasting or touching?

Then bring in the most important layer:
What emotion rises when I imagine this moment fully alive?

If you are visualizing your dream home, imagine the echo of your footsteps across the floor, the warmth of sunlight pouring through the windows, and the quiet hum of peace in the air. Feel the smoothness of the countertop under your hand or the softness of the sofa as you sit down. Smell the scent of your favorite candle as it burns. Taste your morning tea or coffee as if you are already living there.

Let your senses anchor you. Let the emotion rise naturally. When your senses and emotions work together, your nervous system begins to believe the scene. This is not wishing. This is alignment. You are embodying the energy of what you want before it arrives.

Emotional Set Point Journaling

Write down the emotion you want to feel today. Then write one sentence about who you are when you feel that way.

Examples:
"When I feel confident, I trust myself and move with clarity."
"When I feel abundant, I stay open to receiving."
"When I feel peaceful, I respond with intention."
Next, choose one action that honors that emotional state. This anchors your inner shift into your outer behavior.

The Realignment Practice

If a difficult emotion rises during the day, pause and ask:
What story am I telling myself?
Is this story supporting who I am becoming?
What thought would feel even slightly better than this?
Shift gently. Emotional alignment happens through awareness, not force.

Emotion Journal Prompts

Use one to deepen your practice:
"What emotion would my highest self choose right now?"
"What emotion aligns with the life I am creating?"
"What thought created the emotion I am feeling?"
"When do I feel most connected to my desires?"

When Emotional Alignment Feels Hard

Some days, feeling good will feel out of reach. On those days, acknowledge the emotion without judging it. Take a breath. Release the story behind it. Choose one softer thought. Emotional alignment is a series of gentle returns.

The Emotion Flow
To bring this practice together, follow this simple sequence:
- Visualize your desire with full sensory detail and feel the matching emotion.
- Define your emotional set point for the day.
- Choose one aligned action.
- Return to your realignment practice when needed.

Practicing emotion in this intentional way aligns your vibration with the future you are creating and helps you embody the version of yourself who expects your desires to unfold.

Elevation
Elevation is about embodiment. It is who you choose to be every single day. It is the version of you that shows up with intention instead of reaction. Elevation asks you to look at yourself honestly and ask, "Am I thinking like my highest self? Am I speaking like my highest self? Am I moving through the world in a way that reflects who I am becoming?"

Your highest self is not something you wait to meet. It is someone you begin practicing today.

Elevation is also about deliberately choosing your thoughts and emotions. This does not mean forcing yourself to be positive or pretending everything is fine. Elevation is not performance. It is awareness. It is noticing what you are entertaining in your mind and deciding whether it aligns with the version of you who already has what you want. When you elevate your thoughts, you elevate your choices. When you elevate your choices, you elevate your life.

Most people wait for life to shift before they shift. Elevation teaches you to shift first. When you consistently choose thoughts that empower you, emotions that support you, and decisions that honor you, you become a clear match to the reality you desire. You stop waiting for external change and start creating internal alignment.

Elevation is also the practice of stillness. Silent meditation is a portal to higher consciousness, a doorway to the 5D and the realm of the superconscious. In that space, you access guidance and wisdom that cannot be reached through thought alone. Stillness helps you connect with your intuition, your higher self, and the energy of Source. It helps you rise above the noise of the world and tune into the clarity within you.

When you take time to quiet your mind and sit with your breath, your being, and your intention, you elevate your entire frequency. You step out of survival mode and into creation mode. You begin to hear what you need to hear, see what you need to see, and feel what you need to feel in order to move forward with confidence and ease. Elevation is the embodiment of your future self in the present moment.

This is where transformation becomes natural. The more you practice being aligned with your highest self, the more your life begins to reshape itself around that identity. Elevation is not a moment. It is a lifestyle. It is the daily choice to rise.

The Elevation Practice
Elevation is embodiment. It is the daily choice to think, feel, and show up as the version of yourself who already has what they desire. When you elevate your energy from within, your life begins to shift in response. This practice helps you embody your highest self, raise your energetic standard, and connect with the deeper guidance available through stillness.

Silent Meditation for Higher Alignment

Sit comfortably with your spine tall and your hands resting gently in your lap. Close your eyes and breathe naturally. Allow your mind to settle without trying to control your thoughts. If the mind becomes busy, simply notice it and return your focus to your breath.

This stillness is not about forcing quiet. It is about creating space. Silent meditation is a practice of connecting with your higher self, your intuitive wisdom, and the superconscious. In this space, clarity rises, inspired ideas surface, and your energy elevates. Spend a few minutes here and allow your awareness to soften, expand, and open. Any thought, word, image, or nudge that appears is meaningful and often reveals guidance.

Identity Embodiment Journaling

When your meditation is complete, begin your journaling by writing down any insights, ideas, or intuitive messages that came through during your silence. These may be subtle or unexpected, but they are part of your alignment and often reveal your next right step.

Then write down the qualities of your elevated self. Focus on who you are becoming, not who you have been.

Ask yourself:
Who is my elevated self today?
How does this version of me think?
How does this version of me speak?
How does this version of me make decisions?
What are this version's standards?
How does this version of me move through the world?

Choose one of these qualities to embody today. Small, consistent shifts in identity create powerful transformation.

The Alignment Check-In

Throughout the day, pause to tune in to your energy. Ask yourself:

Is my current thought elevating me?
Is this feeling aligned with who I am becoming?
Is this choice honoring my highest self?
If the answer is no, gently guide yourself back toward alignment.
Elevation is a practice of awareness, not perfection.

Elevation Journal Prompts
Use one prompt to deepen your connection to your elevated self:
What clarity rose during my meditation?
What insight or idea am I meant to act on today?
What is my elevated self guiding me to release?
What action would elevate me today?
What belief am I ready to step out of?
These prompts help you recognize the internal shifts that support the life you are creating.

When Elevation Feels Difficult
Some days, you may feel disconnected from your elevated self. This is normal. In those moments, return to the simplest form of elevation:
Pause.
Breathe.
Choose one elevated thought.

Even a small rise in your perspective can shift your energy in powerful ways.

The Elevation Flow
You can bring this practice together by flowing through the following:

- Spend a few minutes in silent meditation to connect with your higher self.
- Write down any insights, guidance, or ideas that came through.
- Choose one quality of your elevated self to embody today.

Use alignment check-ins throughout the day to stay aware of your energy and choices.

Practicing elevation consistently helps you step into the version of yourself who naturally attracts, receives, and maintains the life you are manifesting.

The G.E.E. Morning Ritual

The morning ritual sets the tone for your entire day. For the strongest results, practice it as close to waking up as possible. In those early moments, your brain is shifting from melatonin to serotonin, which creates a natural window of heightened imagination, deep visual access, and increased subconscious receptivity. This is the ideal state for manifestation work.
Do not check your phone or any devices before completing this ritual. External noise pulls you out of the creative state and makes it harder to drop in.

Begin your day with:

Meditation and Visualization:
Sit comfortably, close your eyes, and begin with a few slow breaths. Step into the scene of the life you are creating. See it clearly. Engage all of your senses. Notice what you would see, hear, smell, taste, and feel if your desire were already real. Let the emotion of that moment rise in your body. Stay here for a few minutes, allowing your imagination to guide your energy into alignment.

Stillness and Insight:
After your visualization, allow yourself to rest in quiet awareness. Do not force your mind to be silent. Simply let your thoughts settle. If insights, nudges, or intuitive ideas begin to surface, trust them. This is the elevation stage of your ritual, where guidance, clarity,

and direction can appear naturally. Stay here for another moment before opening your eyes.

Journaling and Gratitude:
Once your meditation is complete, begin journaling. Write down any insights or ideas that surfaced during your stillness. Then write three to five things you are grateful for, including at least one thing you are calling in but stated in the present tense. Close your eyes briefly and feel appreciation for what already exists and for what is becoming. Gratitude anchors the energy you created during your meditation and helps you carry it into your day.

This morning ritual aligns your mind, balances your emotions, and elevates your energy before the world has a chance to impact your vibration. It prepares you to move through the day as the version of yourself who expects alignment, opportunities, and expansion.

The G.E.E. Evening Ritual

Your evening ritual supports the subconscious mind, the part of you that continues creating long after you have closed your eyes. What you focus on before sleep becomes the material your mind processes throughout the night, so this ritual is designed to help you release the day, realign your energy, and drift into rest with intention.

End your day with:

Journaling and Reflection:
Begin by writing a few thoughts from your day. Acknowledge your wins, moments of alignment, and anything you are proud of. If challenges came up, note them without judgment. This reflection helps you process your experiences rather than carry them into sleep. Then end your journaling with one thing you are grateful for from the day. Gratitude softens the mind and signals completion.

Visualization:
Close your eyes and bring your desire to mind. See it clearly without strain. Engage your senses and allow the scene to unfold naturally. Feel the emotion of having it now, the relief, the joy, the ease, the confidence. Evening visualization does not need to be long; it simply needs to be felt. Let this be a gentle return to your intention.

Silent Meditation or Mantra:
After visualizing, rest in stillness. Let your breath slow and your mind quiet. This is your receptive state, where your subconscious begins absorbing everything you feed it through reflection and visualization.

If you prefer, you can replace silent meditation with a soft mantra repeated internally as you drift off. A simple phrase like "I have $500," "Money flows to me easily," or "All my posts go viral," trains your subconscious to accept that idea as fact.

Another powerful option is falling asleep to your own recorded affirmations. Hearing your voice repeating the identity you are stepping into reinforces the belief on a deep level and effortlessly reprograms your mind while you sleep.

This evening ritual closes your day with clarity, alignment, and intention. It gently guides your subconscious into the frequency of receiving, allowing you to fall asleep as the version of yourself who knows abundance, ease, and manifestation is already in motion.

When you live the G.E.E. Framework, you begin to shift from hoping to creating, from wishing to becoming, from waiting to aligning. Gratitude opens your heart, emotion activates your desire, and elevation calls you into the highest expression of who you are meant to be. This framework is not just a practice; it is a way of living that empowers you to show up every day as the creator of your reality. And now that you understand how to align your internal world, it is time to witness what this alignment looks like in action. In the next chapter, Driving My Dreams Into Reality, I will take you into one of the most powerful manifestations of my life, a journey that shows exactly how these principles come together to turn a vision into something you can touch, feel, and drive off the lot with complete certainty.

Chapter 6: Driving Your Dreams into Reality

Manifestation isn't just about dreaming up a shiny new life; it's about becoming a vibrational match to the vision you hold. It's about aligning your thoughts, emotions, and energy with the outcome you desire. In this chapter, I'm pulling back the curtain and sharing one of my most personal manifestations: the journey of calling in a new car. And let me be clear: this wasn't just about getting from point A to point B. It was a spiritual initiation and a test of trust, patience, gratitude, and deep inner knowing.

Back in 2013, I was rolling around in a 1998 Ford Taurus. On the outside, the car looked shiny and put together. But under the hood? Baby, it was very much...drama. That car tested me in every way possible: financially, emotionally, and energetically. As a single mom navigating life's pressures, I felt the weight of every unexpected repair, every dollar stretched, every silent prayer whispered over the steering wheel. But instead of sinking into frustration, I made a decision. I decided to choose gratitude.

Gratitude wasn't always easy, but it was always necessary. Every morning, without fail, I listed ten things I was grateful for. And every single day, the Taurus made the list. Not because it was perfect, it wasn't. But because it was mine. It moved. It worked just enough to get me to where I needed to go. It was doing its best with what it had, and honestly, so was I.

I would literally rub the dashboard as if it were sacred. "I love you so much," I'd whisper. "Thank you, thank you, thank you for getting me to work." That was my ritual. My offering. It was part of how I kept my frequency in check. Even when the A/C gave out in the middle of summer, or when I coasted into the parking lot on fumes and a prayer.

But here's the thing: every time I chose appreciation over annoyance, I was casting a vote for abundance. Every time I looked at that car and said "thank you" instead of "I can't stand this thing," I was rewriting my energy. I wasn't just a woman with an unreliable car. I was a woman preparing for her upgrade.

Gratitude shifted the lens. My circumstances didn't magically change overnight, but my vibration did. And that shift? That's what opened the door for a new chapter to unfold.

A Vision Takes Shape

One quiet morning at the office, I found myself alone, tucked into a sacred stillness that wrapped around me like a warm blanket. It was the perfect moment to dive into my gratitude practice, and as I began to write, something unexpected happened.

Instead of only thanking my car for what it was already doing, I started giving thanks for the things it couldn't yet do. I wrote with conviction, pouring my heart into the page: "Thank you for the smooth ride. Thank you for the working A/C. Thank you for letting me drive across state lines without a second thought." The words flowed effortlessly, but the emotions behind them ran deep. Before I knew it, tears were streaming down my face. This wasn't just gratitude for what was. This was gratitude for what was coming. I felt it in every fiber of my being.

And then it happened: a shift. Like the universe pressed play on a movie that was already waiting for me, I wasn't just visualizing anymore. I was there. I saw myself behind the wheel of a sleek, beautiful car. I could feel the steering wheel in my palms as my fingers comfortably gripped the wheel. I could hear the quiet hum of the engine, and sense the freedom in my chest as I cruised with the windows down and the music up. It felt real, like I had already arrived.

I wasn't wishing. I wasn't hoping. I was living it. My energy had matched the moment, and my imagination became the bridge between what was and what was already becoming. The moment wasn't just a visualization. It was a full-body alignment experience. Gratitude had opened the door. Emotion walked me through it. And something clicked so powerfully inside me, I knew without a doubt my new car was already mine. It was just a matter of time before the rest of the world caught up.

In my mind, I wasn't driving that old Taurus anymore. I was behind the wheel of a sleek black Honda or Toyota, gliding down the highway with ease. An Adele song played on the radio, the kind that hits your soul and makes you feel unstoppable.

I could feel the leather seats beneath me, smell that brand-new car scent, and see the sunlight bouncing off the glossy hood as I drove. It didn't feel like imagination. It felt real. My body tingled with excitement. My heart raced. It was as if I had slipped out of my current reality and into another. I had fallen into a reality where everything I had been visualizing had already come to life.

Caught up in that rush of certainty, I picked up the phone and called my mother. "I'm getting a new car," I blurted out, my voice overflowing with joy. She laughed softly, half encouraging, half cautious, knowing my finances were tight. But I didn't care about the details. I wasn't wondering how it would happen. I just knew that it would.

A short time later, she called me back, her voice filled with disbelief. "You're not going to believe this," she said. "Right after we hung up, a commercial came on for a contest to win a brand-new Honda, and it's black." I got chills. The same car I had just seen so vividly in my mind had appeared on her television.

The contest entry is in-person only at a mall that was quite a drive from where I lived, and my Taurus wasn't exactly road-trip material. So I asked my mom if she'd drive me, and she agreed. It felt like something was aligning. The universe had just opened a door, and all I had to do was walk through it.

Setting the Wheels of Manifestation in Motion

When we arrived at the mall, my eyes were immediately drawn to the contest car on display, a sleek, silver, two-door Honda Civic. It wasn't just any Civic; it was a sporty, top-of-the-line model with all the bells and whistles. The futuristic interior was a far cry from my Taurus. The dashboard lights glowed with sophistication, and the modern controls felt like they belonged in a luxury spaceship rather than an ordinary car. Just taking in the sight of it gave me a rush of excitement, and I could feel my energy vibrating with possibility.

When it was my turn to sit in the car, I slid into the driver's seat and fully immersed myself in the experience. I ran my hands over the steering wheel, feeling the smooth leather beneath my fingers. I inhaled deeply, letting the intoxicating scent of a brand-new car fill my senses. My imagination ran wild. I could *hear* Adele's "Set Fire to the Rain" playing on the stereo, *feel* the smooth ride as I cruised down the highway, and envision the confidence I'd exude behind the wheel of this car. The moment was electric.

My mother, who had been cheering me on the entire time, snapped photos of me sitting in the driver's seat. Those photos became treasures. When we returned home, I looked at them daily, using them to keep my vision alive. I wasn't just daydreaming; I was setting the wheels of manifestation in motion.

Back at home, I took my practice to the next level by creating a vision board. While the contest car was beautiful, my heart is set on a black car like the one in my vision. I found and printed pictures of sleek black Hondas and Toyotas and glued them onto my board. Underneath the images, I wrote affirmations like, "Thank you, thank you, thank you for my new car!" Each time I looked at the board, I felt gratitude and excitement as though the car was already mine. I placed it somewhere I could see every day, so my vision remained vivid and alive in my mind.

Daily Manifestation Practices: Aligning with My Desire

At the time, I was practicing Nichiren Buddhism, chanting Nam Myoho Renge Kyo twice a day. During my chanting sessions, I focused on the image of my new car. The rhythm of the chant elevated my vibration, and I felt deeply connected to my vision.

Every day, I set aside time to manifest my dream car.

My routine included:

Gratitude Journaling: Writing 10 things I was grateful for daily, including my Taurus and the brand new Honda I was calling in.

Visualization: Closing my eyes and imagining myself driving the Honda, complete with vivid details like the smell of leather and the sound of Adele on the radio.

Inspired Actions: I created a pretend title application and bill of sale for a black Honda Accord using a VIN I'd found online. I also took numerous pictures of the interior and exterior of my Taurus and posted them on Craigslist to sell the car, which solidified my belief that the new car was already mine.

Challenges and Tests of Faith: Staying Aligned Through the Storm

Surprise! My car broke down yet again. By this point, it had become a regular occurrence, and, as usual, I didn't have the money to fix it. I had $30 in my bank account, $1 in my wallet, and an unwavering sense of gratitude. Sitting on my bed, I smiled to myself, knowing deep down that I was getting closer to manifesting my new car. Despite the circumstances, I felt optimistic and aligned.

I decided to make the most of what I had. I pulled the single dollar from my wallet and imagined it was a $100 bill. I rubbed it between my hands, holding it high above my head, and pictured $100 bills fluttering down like confetti. This playful moment of imagination filled me with laughter and joy, helping me maintain a high vibration. After tucking the dollar back into my wallet, I headed to my parents' house, where my father would look the car over to see what it needed this time.

On the way to my parents' house, I received a call from a friend who asked to borrow $25. I paused for a moment, remembering that I had only $30 in my account and that my car repair was an imminent expense. Still, I understood an essential truth about abundance: to receive, you must first give. I agreed without hesitation, trusting the process. I reminded myself of a mantra I often used: Money comes easily and frequently. Feeling abundant, I sent the $25 and continued my journey, focusing on gratitude and the certainty that everything would work out.

When I arrived, my father inspected the car and made a few calls. He let me know that the repair would cost $80. Traditionally, I'd ask him for money, and he'd respond with his signature, "Nope." But this time, when I asked if I could borrow the money, he surprised me. With a simple, "Yup," and proceeded to hand me a $100 bill. I was stunned and overjoyed. Only 30 minutes earlier, I had envisioned holding a $100 bill, and now it was in my hand. This moment felt like magic, a powerful reminder of how quickly things can manifest when you stay aligned.

While picking up the car part from the auto parts store, I decided to purchase a Honda keychain. As a regular at the store, the staff knew me well, and the Sales Associate couldn't resist teasing me about the keychain. "Honda? Man, you drive a Ford!" he said with a laugh. I smiled confidently and replied, "Not for long." I left the store feeling even more connected to my vision, as though each step was guiding me closer to my goal.

Later that day, I took my daughter to a doctor's appointment. We had been to this office twice before, and there had never been a co-pay. But when I reached the check-in desk, the Medical Receptionist informed me that a $45 co-pay was due. I didn't flinch. Without a second thought, I pulled out my checkbook and wrote the check, confident that the universe would replenish the funds.

As I waited, I pulled out my dollar bill again, rubbing it between my hands above my head, imagining once more that money was raining down on me. I looked around the waiting room and let my imagination expand further. I visualized handing each person a $50 bill and seeing their gratitude as they received it. This playful exercise kept my vibration high and reminded me of my inherent abundance. With little else to do, I rummaged through my purse and stumbled upon a scratch-off ticket I had scratched weeks earlier. At the time, I thought it was a loser, but out of curiosity, I looked at it again. To my surprise, it was a $45 winner, the exact amount of the co-pay! I couldn't help but laugh, marveling at how the universe always seemed to show up in unexpected ways.

The manifestations didn't stop there. The very next day, the friend who borrowed $25 returned it, adding an extra $15 as a gesture of gratitude. The events of those two days reinforced an important lesson: I didn't need to know how or where the money would come from; I only needed to trust that it existed and remain aligned with gratitude and faith. By ignoring the limitations of my current reality and focusing on the possibilities in my imagination, the money I needed appeared, not once but twice, within minutes.

Through all of this, I stayed connected to my vision of the new car. Despite the challenges, I held onto the belief that it was already mine, and the universe continued to respond to my faith and alignment.

The First Test Drive: Feeling the Vision Come to Life

I knew I needed to experience the feeling of driving a car similar to the one I envisioned. I knew it wasn't just about thinking or visualizing; it was about bringing the experience into my reality to amplify my belief. I decided to visit the dealership to test drive a Honda Civic.

When I arrived, I confidently told the salesman I didn't need financing because someone else was buying the car for me. This statement wasn't about deceiving him; it was about ensuring my mindset remained focused on abundance and not lack. Without hesitation, he nodded and walked off to fetch the car I would take on the test drive.

Imagine my elation when I saw him pull around in a shiny black Honda Civic. It was sleek and beautiful, almost identical to the car I had been visualizing for weeks. My heart raced with excitement as the vision in my mind became tangible and real before me. I couldn't help but smile as I slid into the driver's seat, gripping the steering wheel and inhaling the familiar new car scent. It was like stepping into a scene I had already lived in my imagination.

I drove off the lot alone, and as I took to the road, a wave of joy and alignment washed over me. I played Adele's "Set Fire to the

Rain" on the radio, just as I had envisioned, and it brought my visualization to life. The smooth ride and luxurious feel of the black Civic solidified my belief that this car, or something even better, was on its way to me. At that moment, it felt like I was already living my manifestation.

To anchor the experience, I recorded a video of myself driving the car. In the video, with Adele playing in the background, I said, "This is me driving my new car." That short clip became a source of inspiration, something I watched repeatedly whenever doubt crept in. Each time I pressed play, it reignited my faith, filled me with gratitude, and kept my energy aligned with my dream.

Halfway through the process, I received news that I hadn't won the Honda Civic contest. The sting of disappointment was real. For a brief moment, doubt tried to creep in, whispering questions like, What if this isn't meant to be? What if I'm wrong? But I quickly shifted my focus. I reminded myself that the contest was just one potential avenue for my manifestation, not the only one. The black Honda I envisioned was still out there, waiting for me. I just needed to stay aligned and trust the process.

Later that evening, as I settled in at home, I turned on my TV. I only had access to a few local channels, and there wasn't usually much to watch. But this night was different. To my amazement, Adele was performing live, singing "Set Fire to the Rain", the exact song I had been playing during my visualizations and the first test drive. Tears welled up in my eyes as I sat there, overwhelmed with gratitude and awe.

I knew in my heart that this wasn't a coincidence; it was a sign from the universe, a nudge to remind me that my manifestation was still on its way. The contest may not have been the path, but the destination hadn't changed. The black Honda, my black

Honda, was coming to me. This moment reignited my faith and reaffirmed my belief that the universe was orchestrating something even better than I could imagine.

From that point forward, I leaned into trust with even more confidence. I reminded myself that setbacks are often setups for greater things. The key was to remain open to possibilities, keep my vibration high, and continue acting in alignment with my vision.

The Dealership Visit: Two Cars, One Choice

By the time I decided to visit the dealership to get my approval, I was about 20 days into my manifestation process. I had been consistent with my gratitude practices, journaling, meditating, and maintaining a high vibration. Each day, I focused on feeling good and embodying the energy of someone who already had their dream car. On the surface, my circumstances hadn't changed; my credit was horrible, I had zero savings, and I didn't have a clear path to financing a car. In the 3D, nothing aligned with getting approved for a car loan, but I refused to let that deter me. I knew that the universe does not work through logic; it works through alignment, faith, and consistency.

I decided to visit the dealership when I felt energetically ready. There was no particular reason I chose that day; it simply felt right. I also chose a different dealership from the one where I test-drove the Civic. As I walked into the showroom, I carried my belief like armor, reminding myself that my car was already mine in the 4D.

The salesman reviewed my financial details and said, "I have two cars you can choose from." Then came the inevitable question: "How much can you put down?" Without hesitation, I confidently said, "$2500," even though I had no idea where the money would come from. At that moment, it wasn't about what I had in my bank account; it was about staying in alignment with abundance. Of course, the salesman asked where the money would come from. I blinked a few times, searching for an answer, before finally saying, "I can get it from my 401k." With that, we moved on to the test drive.

The first car he showed me was a silver Honda Civic. This car, however, was nothing like the sleek, sporty silver Civic from the contest. It was a very basic four-door model with standard features, and it didn't evoke the excitement I'd felt during my earlier test drive. As I got behind the wheel, I tried to remain optimistic, but something about the experience felt off. The car felt cramped, uninspiring, disappointing, and completely misaligned with the vision I had so clearly held in mind.

As I drove down the road, an uneasy feeling settled in my chest. The Civic isn't the car I had visualized. It isn't my car. I turned to the salesman and said, "This isn't my car." He laughed and replied, "It's better than that thing you drove in here!" Though his comment stung, I let it roll off my back. I knew the truth: my perfect car was still waiting for me. I left the dealership that day without any idea what the second car would be, but my belief remained intact. Even as I returned home, I felt an unshakable certainty that the universe was still working in my favor.

The Down Payment Challenge

The day after test-driving the silver Honda Civic, I knew the next step was to secure the down payment I had boldly declared to the salesman: $ 2,500. I wasn't fond of the Civic, but I knew the dealership had another option for me based on having the $2,500. Despite not knowing where the money would come from, I was determined to stay aligned with my vision. The most obvious solution was to take a loan from my 401k, so I made the call to explore my options.

The representative informed me that to qualify for a 401k hardship loan, I needed to provide proof of a financial hardship. One qualifying scenario was an eviction notice. Gratefully, I wasn't facing eviction, but this also meant I didn't automatically meet the company's criteria for accessing the funds. As I hung up the phone, I felt a wave of frustration. For a brief moment, I wondered how this challenge would resolve. But then, I remembered what I'd been practicing throughout the process: maintaining gratitude and focusing on the result, not the obstacles.

Within minutes, I received a call from the same friend who had earlier borrowed $25. The timing felt divinely orchestrated, as I hadn't spoken to him in a few days. We chatted casually, and I nonchalantly mentioned my current situation, explaining that I needed a specific document to qualify for the loan. Without missing a beat, he said, "I can get you the document you need."

This friend happened to be a landlord and had access to the exact type of form required. Within moments, he emailed me the document. I submitted it to the 401k company, and within 48 hours, the loan was approved. While the funds wouldn't be deposited into my account right away, I knew this was a breakthrough.

That afternoon, however, the universe decided to test my faith once again. I was preparing to run a quick errand to the store, but when I turned the key in the ignition, my car refused to start. The engine was silent, and for a moment, I felt frustration creeping in. But I caught myself. I took a deep breath, stepped out of the car, locked the door, and began walking to the store instead. With each step, I silently repeated, "Thank you for my new car." It wasn't just an affirmation; it was a choice to focus on gratitude and abundance rather than lack.

That evening, I began to feel the weight of the day's challenges. Sitting at my parents' house, where I had to stay so they could help me get to work, I found myself questioning everything. Was I crazy for believing in something that seemed so impossible? Was this all just wishful thinking? The doubt began to take root, and I could feel my vibration sinking.

Just as the negativity began to overwhelm me, the universe intervened once again. My phone rang, and it was one of my silliest, most lighthearted friends. For the next hour, we laughed hysterically about anything and everything. The conversation completely shifted my energy, pulling me out of doubt and back into joy, gratitude, and belief. By the time I hung up, I had renewed my faith and remembered that the universe always has a way of realigning us when we're open to receiving.

The challenges of that day became powerful lessons in resilience. They reminded me that manifestation isn't about avoiding obstacles, it's about choosing alignment despite them. With my vibration restored and the 401k loan approved, I felt a renewed sense of momentum. The pieces were falling into place, and I knew I was closer than ever to driving away in the car I had envisioned.

The Black Accord Appears

The day after my 401k loan was approved, I felt an undeniable shift in my energy. Knowing the down payment had been secured gave me renewed confidence. For the first time, I truly felt like my dream car was within reach. While at work that day, I decided to browse the dealership's website for inspiration, not expecting to see much. But as soon as the homepage loaded, my heart skipped a beat. There it was: a shiny black Honda Accord, featured prominently at the top of the page.

My breath caught in my chest. The sleek design, the deep black finish, it was everything I had envisioned and more. The moment I saw it, I knew. That's my car. It wasn't just a thought; it was a deep, inner knowing that this was the car I had been manifesting all along. The vision I'd held so clearly in my mind had materialized on the screen in front of me.

Without hesitation, I picked up the phone and called the salesman I'd been working with. Barely able to contain my excitement, I asked him about the black Accord on the website. His response was casual, almost nonchalant: "Oh yeah, that was the other car I was going to show you."

I could barely stay seated at my desk. My excitement was bubbling over. This is it, I thought. This is the car I've been waiting for. The black Honda Accord wasn't just a car; it was the physical manifestation of all the gratitude, belief, and alignment I had cultivated over the past three weeks.

In that moment, everything felt like it was clicking into place. The universe had been guiding me to this car all along, and I knew I was just one step away from making it mine.

The Moment of Manifestation

The moment I got off work that day, I headed straight to the dealership, my anticipation building with every mile. When I arrived, the salesman didn't lead me to the lot. Instead, he escorted me to the service garage, where I caught my first glimpse of the car. There it was, a shiny black Honda Accord, freshly washed and gleaming under the garage lights. My heart skipped a beat. This was the car I had been manifesting, the one

I had envisioned so vividly in my mind.

As I moved toward the car, I noticed something unexpected. Several dealership employees had gathered around, chatting and watching as my vehicle was prepped. The doors were open, the freshly cleaned interior was on display, and the moment felt surreal. It was as if I had stepped onto the set of a game show and was racing toward the grand prize I had just won. I couldn't help but exclaim to the salesman, "That's my car!" The excitement in my voice was palpable, and the energy in the garage was electric.

The moment is filled with such joy and alignment that I couldn't resist adding a bit of humor. "The difference between the Civic and the Accord took me from crawlin' to ballin'!" I joked. The employees who had gathered nearby burst into laughter, sharing in my excitement. They had no idea about the manifestation journey that had brought me to this exact moment, but it felt as though they were celebrating with me nonetheless.

The salesman smiled and handed me the keys for a test drive. Sliding into the driver's seat was like stepping into a dream come true. The interior was pristine, the spacious design felt luxurious, and the handling was smooth and effortless.

Everything about the experience confirmed what I already knew: this was the car I had been manifesting. After only a few seconds in the driver's seat, I turned to the salesman and confidently declared, "Yup…this is it!"

Even though the 401k funds weren't in my account, the salesman accepted a post-dated check, trusting that everything would come together. As I drove off the lot in my brand-new car, I felt a deep sense of gratitude, fulfillment, and alignment.

The car wasn't technically brand new, it was five years old with less than 30,000 miles on it, practically new in my eyes. The sleek design, the deep black finish, and the like-new condition made it feel perfect. I knew, without a doubt, that this was my car.

Later that evening, when I checked the car's VIN, I was stunned to discover that it matched the number I had written on my pretend title application weeks earlier. That detail was so specific, so aligned, that it brought me to tears. It was undeniable proof that the universe had orchestrated every step of this process, turning my vision into reality in the most perfect way.

The next day, I decided to go to my favorite auto parts store for an air freshener for my new car. As I approached the counter, my favorite store associate was surprised to see me, and he said, "What happened, now?!?"
I smiled at him, held up my Honda keychain, and said, "This happened."

His eyes got big, and his disbelief was evident. So much so that he walked away from an open register drawer and walked outside with me so he could see for himself. The Sales Associate was just as excited as I was, and his manager had to come outside to remind him that he had walked away from a customer in the middle of a transaction. In his reaction, I saw my own transformation reflected back, proof that when your belief shifts, your entire world shifts with it.

From Energy to Expansion

The journey to manifesting my car was far more than just acquiring a new vehicle; it was a transformative experience that deepened my understanding of alignment, gratitude, and unwavering belief. Each step, including visualizing the car to taking inspired actions, was powered by the energy I emitted into the universe. That energy, my vibration, became the cornerstone of my manifestation process. It wasn't just about the physical actions I took; it was about the state of being I maintained, no matter the external challenges.

Every test along the way reinforced an undeniable truth: manifestation isn't about wishing or hoping; it's about mastering your vibration. Your thoughts, emotions, and beliefs create the energetic blueprint for your reality. When I sat on my bed, smiling at my $1 bill; when I imagined $100 bills raining down; and when I confidently told the salesman I had $2500 for a down payment, despite not yet knowing how, I was aligning my vibration with abundance, trust, and gratitude.

Even in moments of doubt, like learning I hadn't won the contest or navigating the 401k approval process, I chose to focus on what I wanted rather than what I lacked. Each challenge reminded me to stay aligned with the end result, not the obstacles. My friend providing the necessary documentation or the VIN matching the one I had written on my pretend title application was an explicit confirmation from the universe: When you master your vibration, you become a magnet for your desires.

Manifestation isn't just about what you do; it's about the energy behind your actions. Every thought, every feeling, and every decision contributes to your vibration, determining how effortlessly your desires flow into your reality. My journey taught me that the universe responds not to what you wish for but to who you become in the process. By aligning my energy with my dream, I didn't just manifest a car; I became the person who naturally attracts abundance. That's what it means to Manifest

Like a G.E.E., to show up with gratitude, stay anchored in elevated emotion, and embody the version of you that already has it all.

As we move forward into Part 2: Deepening Understanding, we'll explore the foundational principles that amplify your manifestation practice. Together, we'll delve into the power of vibration, uncover the science behind manifestation, and learn how to overcome limiting beliefs that may be silently blocking your success. By deepening your understanding of these principles, you'll gain the tools to elevate your vibration and align more profoundly with your dreams, setting the stage for even greater transformations.

Part 2: Deepening Understanding

Chapter 7: The Power of Vibration

Energy flows where attention goes, and the energy you emit into the universe is the vibration that shapes your reality. From the tiniest atom to the vast expanse of the cosmos, everything vibrates at its own unique frequency, including your thoughts, emotions, and beliefs. The key to creating the life you desire is understanding and mastering your vibration.

In this chapter, we'll dive deeper into the principles of the Law of Vibration, explore how it works as the foundation of manifestation, and uncover practical ways to align your vibration with your goals. By the end, you'll see that managing your vibration is not just a spiritual concept; it's a practical tool for transforming your life.

What is the Law of Vibration?

The Law of Vibration is the principle that underpins all creation. It states that everything in existence is in a constant state of motion, vibrating at its own frequency. This vibration determines the form, behavior, and interactions of all matter and energy in the universe.

Bruce Lipton discovered that identical stem cells could become muscle, bone, or fat depending on their environment, not on their genes. He later taught that, just as those cells do, your thoughts and emotions (your vibration) shape your reality.

Imagine you're standing next to a tuning fork. When struck, the tuning fork emits a specific vibration, and if another tuning fork nearby vibrates at the same frequency, it will resonate in harmony. The universe operates the same way: similar vibrations attract each other.

Your thoughts and emotions are no different. They emit frequencies that interact with the vibrations of people, circumstances, and opportunities in your life. Here's a relatable example: Have you ever had a day when you felt amazing, and everything seemed to go your way? That's because your high vibration attracted experiences that matched your energy. Conversely, when you're in a bad mood, it often feels like one thing after another goes wrong. That's the Law of Vibration in action.

But here's the empowering truth: You are not a passive participant in this process. You can consciously direct your vibration and attract the experiences you desire. Your vibration is the invisible force behind everything you experience. It acts like a tuning fork, broadcasting your energy into the universe and attracting frequencies that match it.

Your vibration acts as a filter for your reality. For example:
- If you're vibrating at a high frequency, you'll notice opportunities, solutions, and synchronicities that align with your goals.
- If you're vibrating at a low frequency, you're more likely to focus on obstacles, problems, and setbacks.

Your vibrational state also influences your behavior:
- When you're in a high-vibe state, you feel inspired, confident, and motivated to take action.
- When you're in a low-vibe state, you're more likely to procrastinate, second-guess yourself, or give up.

Understanding this connection is critical because it shows that shifting your vibration isn't just about feeling good; it's about aligning your energy with the actions and outcomes that support your goals.

So, how do you know your vibrational state? Becoming aware of your vibration is the first step to mastering it. Your emotions are your most significant indicator of your current vibrational state. Think of them as your personal GPS, constantly providing feedback on your alignment with your desires.

Signs You're in a High-Vibration State
- Emotional Indicators: You feel joyful, grateful, or excited. There's a sense of ease and flow in your day.
- External Indicators: Things seem to "fall into place." You meet the right people, receive unexpected blessings, or encounter synchronicities that feel like divine guidance.
- Physical Indicators: You have energy, feel light and vibrant, and may even notice improvements in your physical health.

Signs You're in a Low-Vibration State
- Emotional Indicators: You feel anxious, frustrated, or stuck. Negative thoughts dominate your mind.
- External Indicators: You encounter obstacles, delays, or conflicts. It feels like nothing is going your way.
- Physical Indicators: You may feel drained, heavy, or lethargic, with a tendency toward physical discomfort.

How to Raise Your Vibration
Raising your vibration doesn't require drastic changes. Small, consistent actions can have a profound impact on your energy. Here are some practical ways to elevate your vibration:

Gratitude
Gratitude is one of the quickest ways to shift your vibration. When you focus on what you're grateful for, you align yourself with the frequency of abundance.

-Practical Tip: Start each day by writing down three things you're grateful for. Feel the gratitude deeply as you reflect on each one.

Askfirmations

When you ask a question, you give your brain a job to do. Unlike a statement, which can feel like a done deal, a question sparks curiosity and opens the door for new solutions and insights. It's like handing your subconscious a mission: *"Go figure this out."* That's why askfirmations are so powerful. Instead of saying, *"I am abundant,"* you ask, *"Why am I so abundant?"* That question sends your mind searching for evidence, rewiring your beliefs along the way.

-Pro Tip: Ask your brain a powerful question. It loves solving problems more than accepting final answers.

Movement and Exercise

Physical activity releases endorphins and boosts your energy. Whether it's dancing, yoga, or a brisk walk, moving your body helps clear stagnant energy and raises your vibration.

- Pro Tip: Choose activities that bring you joy and make you feel alive.

Surround Yourself with High-Vibe People

Energy is contagious. Spend time with people who uplift and inspire you, and limit exposure to negativity.

- Action Step: Join communities or groups that share your values and goals.

Meditation

Meditation helps you quiet your mind, connect with your higher self, and reset your vibration.
- Guided Exercise: Close your eyes, take deep breaths, and visualize a bright light filling your body, raising your energy with

each inhale.

Music and Sound Healing

Sound has a powerful effect on your vibration. Listen to uplifting music, chant affirmations, or explore sound healing with singing bowls or tuning forks.

- Suggestion: Create a playlist of songs that make you feel empowered and play it whenever you need an energy boost.

Your Vibe Is the Bridge: Navigating 3D, 4D, and 5D

Your vibration is more than just how you feel. It's the signal you're sending out and the energy you tune into. It's also the bridge that carries you through the different dimensions of your manifestation journey.

- 3D Reality, Gratitude Grounds You: In the 3D, life is physical. What you see, hear, and touch all feel very real. Your current circumstances shape your vibration here. But this is also where the shift begins. Gratitude becomes your anchor. When you start focusing on what's working instead of what's missing, your energy begins to shift. Let's call this your Outer GEE
- 4D Reality, Emotion Creates: In the 4D, your thoughts and emotions begin to shape your experience. Here is where you tap into your imagination and begin to feel your way into your desires. Visualization, affirmations, and askfirmations raise your vibe and start building the energetic blueprint for what's next. 4D is considered your Inner GEE.
- 5D Reality, Elevation Aligns: In the 5D, you move beyond effort and into ease. You're in full alignment. You trust. You allow. You become the energy of what you desire. Gratitude is no longer just a practice; it's who you are. 5D is the dimension of flow, joy, and divine timing. I like to call this your Higher GEE.

The higher your vibration, the easier it is to shift between dimensions and live in harmony with what you're calling in.

The Power of Vibration and the Science of Manifestation

Vibration is the energetic language of the universe. By aligning your vibration with your desires, you activate the magnetic pull that draws them into your reality. But why does this work? What happens in your mind and body when you elevate your energy?

In the next chapter, The Science of Manifestation, we'll uncover the fascinating connection between spiritual practices like vibration-raising and scientific principles such as neuroplasticity and quantum physics. You'll learn how your brain, emotions, and energy work together to turn your dreams into reality and help you master how to Manifest Like a G.E.E.

Chapter 8: The Science of Manifestation

For centuries, manifestation was viewed through a primarily spiritual lens, a practice of visualizing, believing, and receiving. While these principles remain central, modern science is uncovering fascinating connections between manifestation practices and the workings of the brain and body. By bridging spirituality with neuroscience, we gain a deeper understanding of why manifestation works and how to amplify its effects.

In this chapter, we'll explore the science behind the key dimensions of manifestation, gratitude, emotion, and elevation, and how they align with the brain's natural processes. From rewiring your neural pathways to activating the Reticular Activating System (RAS), these insights will help you understand why your mindset is truly the foundation for your reality.

Neuroplasticity: Rewiring Your Mind for Success

Your brain is not fixed. It's flexible, adaptable, and constantly evolving. This ability to change, called *neuroplasticity*, is one of the most powerful tools in your manifestation toolbox. Every time you think a new thought, feel a new emotion, or practice gratitude, you're creating new neural pathways. Over time, those pathways become your new normal, and your reality begins to shift.

Dr. Joe Dispenza explains this beautifully. He teaches that when you combine intention with elevated emotion, you're not just hoping for a new future, you're wiring it into your brain. The brain doesn't know the difference between a vividly imagined experience and a real one. So when you visualize your desires with feeling, you're rehearsing your future into existence.

Let's break this down through the G.E.E. lens:

Gratitude: Practicing gratitude lights up your brain's reward system. It floods your body with feel-good chemicals like dopamine and starts rewiring your mind to expect positive outcomes.

- Emotion: The glue that holds your vision together. The stronger the emotional charge, the more deeply the experience is encoded into your brain, making your future feel real in the now.
- Elevation: When you align your thoughts and emotions with a higher version of yourself, you raise your frequency and create a new energetic signature that the universe can match.

The RAS: Your Brain's Manifestation Filter

Now let's talk about your Reticular Activating System (RAS). This robust network of neurons acts like a personal assistant for your mind. It filters your reality based on what you focus on. If you are constantly affirming that you are worthy, abundant, and supported, your RAS will begin to notice the people, places, and opportunities that reflect that belief.

Whether you're visualizing your dream home or journaling about your future business, you're not just playing pretend. You're training your brain to recognize, attract, and align with your desires. Keep practicing. Keep imagining. Keep feeling it as real. Your brain, your body, and the universe are all responding.

Example: In my car manifestation journey, programming my RAS with visualizations and affirmations helped me notice the black Accord on the dealership's website at the perfect moment. Without that mental focus, I might have overlooked it entirely.

Let's break it down: manifestation isn't just a feel-good concept; it's backed by energy, vibration, and real science. Everything in this universe is vibrating. Your thoughts? Vibration. Your emotions? Vibration. Even your body is radiating an energetic frequency at all times. The key is learning how to shift that frequency to match the reality you want to experience.

The Law of Vibration and Quantum Alignment

When you think thoughts of lack, fear, or doubt, your vibration gets low and murky. But when you flood your system with gratitude, elevated emotion, and belief, you raise your frequency and begin to align with abundance. Now the real magic happens. You don't attract what you want; *you attract what's on the frequency at which you are vibrating.*

As Joe Dispenza reminds us, tuning your thoughts and feelings to the frequency of your desired future isn't just wishful thinking; it's embodiment. When you consistently align with that energy, you're not waiting for your future to arrive; you're becoming it now.

Dimensional Vibe Check

- Gratitude (3D): Grounding yourself in appreciation shifts your focus from problems to possibilities.
  - Emotion (4D): When you fuel your vision with emotion, you breathe life into it. That feeling is the signal.
  - Elevation (5D): Tools like meditation, visualization, and heart coherence help lift your energy into alignment, where manifestation becomes flow.

Real-Life Practice:

Start your day by placing your hand over your heart. Breathe deeply and name three things you're genuinely grateful for. Let yourself feel the emotion of it. This one practice can shift your entire frequency and open the door to everything you've been calling in.

The Chemistry of Manifestation

Gratitude and Dopamine
Gratitude activates the brain's reward system, releasing dopamine and serotonin. These chemicals not only make you feel good but also enhance motivation and focus, making it easier to take inspired action toward your goals.

Visualization and Oxytocin
Visualizing your desires while connecting to positive emotions releases oxytocin, the "love hormone." This chemical fosters a sense of trust and openness, helping you surrender to the process without resistance.

Putting the Science into Practice

Daily Gratitude and Reflection
Keep a journal to track moments of gratitude, reinforcing the neural pathways associated with abundance. Over time, this practice helps you stay focused on what's working, rather than what's lacking.

Emotional Rehearsal
Pair your visualizations with elevated emotions. Instead of simply imagining your desire, feel the excitement, joy, or peace it would bring. The stronger the emotional response, the more effectively you program your brain.

Meditation for Coherence
Practice heart-brain coherence by focusing on your heart as you breathe deeply. Combine this with affirmations to create a powerful state of alignment.

Let's revisit the story of manifesting the black Accord. When my car broke down, I could have easily spiraled into fear and frustration. Instead, I used gratitude to elevate my vibration and visualized myself driving the exact car I wanted. This consistent programming of my RAS helped me take aligned action, notice opportunities, and trust the process. Every step of that journey, from creating a pretend title application to meditating daily, was rooted in the science of manifestation, supported by focus, gratitude, and elevated emotion.

Understanding the science of manifestation reveals just how powerful your mind truly is. Practices like visualization, gratitude, and emotional alignment rewire your brain and elevate your vibration, aligning you with your desires on both a spiritual and scientific level. But even with this understanding, hidden barriers like limiting beliefs can still hold you back.

Limiting beliefs act like anchors, keeping you tied to old patterns and preventing you from fully stepping into the life you desire. In the next chapter, Overcoming Limiting Beliefs, we'll explore how to identify and transform these subconscious blocks, clearing the way for the practices you've learned to work at their highest potential.

Chapter 9: Breaking the Chains of Limiting Beliefs

Limiting beliefs are like invisible chains wrapped around your potential. You don't always see them, but you feel them every time you try to dream bigger or move beyond your comfort zone. They show up as doubt, hesitation, procrastination, and fear. Most of the time, we don't even realize we're carrying them. They sneak in from childhood, past failures, societal expectations, or words spoken over us that we unknowingly absorbed as truth.

But here's the truth: those beliefs are not who you are. They're stories, old ones. And you can rewrite them. If you want to manifest a life that feels good and true to your spirit, you have to be willing to question those internal narratives. You have to ask, "Whose voice is this?" and "Does this belief serve the life I'm creating?" Because manifestation is less about pushing and more about aligning. And alignment can't happen when you're dragging around outdated beliefs that contradict your vision.

In this chapter, we're going to get real about how limiting beliefs develop, how they sabotage your manifestations, and how you can flip them into powerful affirmations that actually support your growth. But first, let me take you back to one of the most unforgettable manifestation moments of my life, when I turned pure energy, focus, and belief into $500 in less than an hour.

Manifestation Story: The $500 Breakthrough
Back in 2006, I was a single parent trying to stay afloat. Money was tight, bills were overdue, and the stress was eating at me. That's when I was introduced to The Secret and started exploring the Law of Attraction. Around the same time, I began practicing Nichiren Buddhism, chanting "Nam Myoho Renge

Kyo," a meditative practice that helped me anchor my mind and energy.

One day, I went to a chanting meeting. It wasn't just any meeting; at this meeting, we would chant nonstop for one hour. It was my first time chanting for a full hour straight, and I was determined to make it count. At first, I didn't know what to focus on. But then it hit me: I needed $500 to catch up on some bills.

As I chanted, I didn't just say the words. I visualized the outcome. I pictured the money in my hands. I felt the weight of financial relief. I imagined sitting down with those bills, paying them off, and exhaling deeply. The emotion was real. The gratitude was already present, even before the money showed up. It was a moment of deep alignment, where my intention, feeling, and belief locked into place.

The Immediate Manifestation

Right after the meeting, I went to a friend's house. It was one of those places I could always pop in, unwind, laugh, and enjoy good company. As soon as I pulled into the driveway, one of her family members came outside and asked me to take them to the store.

Now listen, I was tired. I had just come from pouring my soul into that chant and really just wanted to sit still. But I said yes. The store was just a minute away, and I stayed in the car while they went inside. About 10 minutes later, they came back out, hopped in the car, and handed me $500 in cash.

I froze.
"What's this for?" I asked.
They smiled and said, "I'm sure you have some bills to pay. Handle your business."

I'm floored. In less than an hour, I had manifested exactly what I had chanted for. It was one of those moments that changed everything for me. It wasn't just about the money. It was about realizing what happens when belief, energy, and emotion come into harmony.

That day taught me that limiting beliefs can be cracked wide open in an instant. And that the universe really does respond to clarity, emotion, and alignment. But the real lesson came afterward, in a way I didn't expect.

The Lesson on Integrity with Money

The manifestation itself was nothing short of magical. It was a real-time reminder of how powerful energy and belief can be when you're fully aligned. But what happened after that was what changed me the most.

I had every intention of using that $500 to pay off some overdue bills, just like I had visualized during the chant. But instead, I let the excitement take over. I convinced myself it was smart to put the money into what I'll refer to as a 'high-return opportunity' that sounded too good to be true. And it was. It turned out to be a scam.

The money disappeared.

The bills were still there, and I felt disappointed and out of alignment. I had asked the universe for help, received it with precision, and then misused the blessing. That moment made me pause. It showed me that manifestation isn't just about receiving. It's about honoring what you receive and staying in alignment with your original intention.

Money is energy. And when you don't treat that energy with

respect, it stops flowing the way you want it to. For months after that, no matter how much I visualized or journaled, the financial breakthroughs slowed to a crawl. It wasn't until I sat with myself, reflected, and made peace with the decision I had made that things started to shift.

I had to rebuild trust, with money and with myself. I promised to treat every dollar with care and intention moving forward. Once I honored that vow, the abundance returned, flowing with a steady rhythm that felt aligned and peaceful.

Limiting beliefs are like invisible fences. You don't always see them, but they quietly shape your world, keeping you boxed in and second-guessing what's possible. These beliefs aren't truths; they're outdated stories we picked up along the way. Stories like "I'm not good enough," "Money is hard to come by," or "Love never lasts for me." And while they may feel real, they're often rooted in fear, past wounds, and what someone else once told us about who we are.

Most of the time, these beliefs live in the subconscious. That means they can run the show without us even realizing it. They shape the way we think, how we show up in relationships, what we believe we're worth, and how bold we're willing to be. Maybe it came from something you heard in childhood. Perhaps it was a breakup or a job you didn't get. Or maybe you've just been swimming in societal noise that tells you to play small, stay safe, and not expect too much. But just because it's familiar doesn't mean it has to be your truth.

The first shift comes with awareness. Start by getting honest with yourself. Where in your life do you feel stuck, heavy, or like you're constantly hitting a wall? What thoughts pop up when you imagine living your dream life? Listen closely, because those whispers of doubt are often where the most profound transformation begins.

Then ask: Is this belief even true? Who told me this? Have I ever experienced something that proves this wrong? Let's say you've been carrying the belief that money is always hard to come by. But if you really think about it, maybe there was a time you received an unexpected check, or someone treated you without you even asking. That moment right there is evidence. And where there's one moment, there can be many more.

Once you've uncovered the lie, it's time to rewrite the story. Speak life into a new belief. Instead of saying "I'm bad with money," try "I'm learning to manage my money with ease and confidence." Instead of "I don't deserve love," say "I am worthy of deep, lasting love that aligns with who I am." And don't just say it. Feel it. Let it land. Repeat it until your subconscious starts to believe it too.

But we can't stop at words alone. Your new beliefs need action to back them up. If you believe in abundance, give a little, even when you don't feel like you have much. If you believe you're worthy of love, start treating yourself with the same care and softness you want from a partner. When your energy, thoughts, and actions line up, that's when the magic happens.

It's how you take your power back, one belief, one shift, one aligned action at a time.

Practical Exercises to Reprogram Your Mind
Belief Inventory

Pick one area of your life, like finances, health, or relationships. Write down every belief or thought you have about it, without editing or holding back. Then, go through your list and highlight anything negative or limiting. For each one, create a new empowering affirmation that flips the script. Replace "I always struggle with money" with "Abundance flows to me in unexpected ways."

Daily Visualization

Take 5 to 10 minutes each day to see your desired reality in vivid detail. Feel the emotions. Picture the scene. Smell the air, hear the sounds, and step into the version of you who's already living it. Focus on joy, gratitude, and fulfillment as if it's already yours, because energetically, it is.

Gratitude Reframe

When a limiting belief creeps in, gently shift your focus to gratitude. If you feel stressed about money, pause and name three things that money has already helped you with, even if it's just gas in your car, a hot meal, or the roof over your head. Gratitude raises your vibration and rewires your brain to see abundance instead of lack.

Overcoming Limiting Beliefs to Alignment and Trust in the Universe

Releasing limiting beliefs is one of the most powerful moves you can make on your manifestation journey. It's like clearing out energetic clutter so the universe can finally deliver what you've been asking for. As those old doubts and patterns fall away, you naturally align with the energy of what you truly desire. And in that space of alignment, trust begins to rise. You no longer chase or force; you flow.

That $500 manifestation? It was proof of what's possible when belief, emotion, and energy meet. I didn't just ask for the money; I became the version of me who already had it. I felt it. I trusted it. And then the universe came through in a way I never could've scripted. But that moment also taught me a more profound lesson: staying aligned isn't just about what you think or feel, it's also about what you do with what you receive; Integrity matters. Energy responds to truth.

In the next chapter, we'll go even deeper into what it means to align fully, to trust the universe, and to co-create from a place of deep knowing. Because once you're genuinely in flow, your dreams can't help but find their way to you.

Chapter 10: Alignment and Trust in the Universe

Alignment and trust in the universe are the twin pillars of manifestation. They work together to bridge the gap between your desires and their realization. Alignment ensures that your energy matches what you want to attract, while trust lets you let go of doubts, fears, and control, allowing the universe to work its magic. It is how you begin to Manifest Like a G.E.E., by syncing your inner world with your desires and surrendering the rest to divine timing.

In this chapter, we'll explore what alignment truly means, how to cultivate it, and how trusting the universe can lead to miraculous results, even when it feels impossible. I'll also share the story of my green lights manifestation as a powerful example of staying aligned and trusting the process.

Understanding Alignment: A State of Flow

Alignment is when your thoughts, feelings, and actions are in harmony with your desires. Imagine a river flowing effortlessly toward the ocean. When you're in alignment, you're like that river, moving smoothly toward your goals, guided by the natural current of the universe. But what does being out of alignment feel like? It's the opposite. It's like paddling upstream, fighting against the current with frustration, fear, and resistance.

Signs You're in Alignment:
- You feel calm, confident, and centered.
- You're excited about your desires without obsessing over them.
- Synchronicities (or "signs") appear frequently, like seeing repeating numbers or hearing someone mention something you

were thinking about.
- Inspired actions feel natural and effortless, like following a nudge or taking a chance.

How to Cultivate Alignment:
1. Daily Mindfulness Practices: Meditation, gratitude journaling, and affirmations help ground you in the present moment and keep your energy high.
2. Visualize with Feeling: Imagine yourself already living your desired outcome and allow those emotions to flood your being.
3. Release Resistance: Acknowledge and let go of doubts, fears, and limiting beliefs that block your flow.
4. Stay Grateful: Gratitude amplifies alignment by focusing your energy on abundance rather than lack.

Trusting the Universe: Letting Go of the How

Once you've aligned with your desires, the next step is to trust the universe to deliver them in the perfect way and at the perfect time. Trusting the universe is about surrender, releasing control over how and when things will happen.

Why Trust is Key:
- It Prevents Overthinking: Trying to control every detail often leads to frustration and doubt.
- It Keeps You in the Present Moment: Trust allows you to enjoy the journey rather than constantly worrying about the destination.
- It Opens Doors to Miracles: When you let go, you create space for unexpected blessings.

Dr. Carol Dweck, Stanford psychologist and author of "Mindset", reminds us that shifting into a growth mindset is a powerful act of alignment. When we open ourselves to possibility, we create space for trust, allowing the universe to meet us at the level of our belief. That shift? It's a whole G.E.E. vibe: gratitude for where you are, emotion fueling where you're heading, and elevation into who you're becoming.

Personal Story: The Green Lights Manifestation

Let me share a powerful example of alignment and trust in action. It was a summer evening, and I was hanging out with my brother and his friends, having the time of my life. Suddenly, I glanced at my watch and realized I was already running late for my midnight shift at work. Panic set in; I was already on attendance probation, and it looked like there was no way I'd make it on time.

For a split second, I gave in to that panic, but then I remembered something crucial: I am a deliberate creator. I took a deep breath, shook off the fear, and decided to tap into my inner G.E.E. Instead of focusing on the fear of being late, I declared, "Green lights and plenty of time!" over and over again.

As I got in my car, I focused solely on the outcome I wanted: arriving at work on time. I imagined the joy and relief I'd feel when I clocked in just in time, and I kept repeating my affirmation with absolute faith.

And then it happened. Every single traffic light turned green as I approached. One after another, green, green, green! I couldn't believe what I was seeing, and I started laughing hysterically. It felt like the universe was orchestrating a private light show just for me. And this wasn't just four or five lights; this had to be at least 30 traffic lights!

At one point, I did hit a red light, but before I could even fully stop, it turned green again. It was incredible. By the time I arrived at work, I had two minutes to spare. The relief, joy, and empowerment I felt in that moment were unforgettable. I aligned my energy with the outcome I wanted, trusted the universe to handle the rest, and it delivered.

Overcoming Challenges to Alignment

Life isn't always smooth sailing, and staying aligned can feel difficult when challenges arise. Here's how to overcome those moments:

1. Recognize Resistance

Resistance often shows up as frustration, doubt, or a feeling of being "stuck." Acknowledge it without judgment, and then ask yourself: "What's one small step I can take to realign?"

2. Shift Your Focus

When you're out of alignment, it's usually because you're focusing on what you don't want. Pause, take a deep breath, and redirect your attention to what you do want.

3. Use Mantras or Affirmations

Powerful phrases like "Everything is always working out for me" or "I trust the universe to guide me" can help you regain faith and balance.

Actionable Practices for Alignment and Trust

To help you stay aligned and deepen your trust in the universe, try these practices:

1. Morning Alignment Ritual

- Spend 10 minutes visualizing your goals as if they've already manifested.
- Write down three things you're grateful for.
- Set a daily intention, such as "Today, I will approach everything with ease and joy."

2. Letting Go Exercise

- Write down your worries or fears on a piece of paper.
- After acknowledging them, tear up the paper and throw it away

as a symbol of release.

3. Celebrate Small Wins

- Acknowledge and celebrate every small manifestation or sign from the universe, no matter how minor it may seem. Gratitude builds momentum.

Alignment and trust in the universe are your most excellent tools for manifesting the life you desire. When you align your energy with your dreams and trust the process, you open yourself to unlimited possibilities. The green lights story reminds us that miracles happen when we shift our focus, hold unwavering belief, and let the universe take care of the rest. Remember: your job is not to control every detail but to stay aligned, take inspired action, and trust that everything is unfolding perfectly.

Turning Alignment into Action

Alignment and trust are the foundation of manifestation, allowing you to stay connected to your desires and open to the universe's guidance. When your thoughts, emotions, and energy are in harmony, you become a magnet for the life you want to create.

But manifestation doesn't stop at alignment; it also requires movement. Action is the bridge between your inner vision and your outer reality. In the next section, Taking Action, we'll explore how to combine inspired steps with trust and alignment to create powerful momentum toward your dreams.

Part 3: Taking Action

Chapter 11: Taking Inspired Action

Manifestation isn't just about thinking, feeling, or visualizing; it's about taking action. But not just any action: inspired action. Inspired action is the bridge between your desires and their manifestation in the physical world.

In this chapter, we'll explore what inspired action means, how to recognize it, and how to overcome resistance to act. You'll learn to trust your intuition, follow the signs, and create momentum toward your dreams.

What is Inspired Action?

Inspired action feels natural, exciting, and aligned with your desires. It's different from forced or obligatory action because it comes from a place of flow and intuition rather than pressure or fear.

Key Characteristics of Inspired Action
1. It Feels Right: Inspired actions often feel like a "hell yes!" rather than a reluctant "I guess I should."
2. It Comes with Clarity: You may suddenly know exactly what to do next, even if you didn't have a plan moments before.
3. It Feels Energizing: Rather than draining you, inspired action fills you with excitement and motivation.
4. It Aligns with Your Vision: It supports your goals and feels like a step in the right direction.

How to Recognize Inspired Action
Recognizing inspired action requires tuning into your intuition and being open to signs from the universe.

1. Trust Your Intuition
Your intuition is your internal compass. It speaks to you through gut feelings, flashes of insight, or a deep sense of knowing. When something feels right, it usually is.
Example: You might feel an urge to reach out to someone you haven't spoken to in years, only to discover they have the perfect opportunity for you.

2. Pay Attention to Signs
The universe communicates with you through synchronicities, unexpected opportunities, and repeating patterns. If you keep seeing or hearing something that relates to your goal, it's a nudge to take action.
Example: If you're manifesting a career change and keep stumbling across job postings in your dream industry, it's a sign to apply.

3. Listen to Your Emotions
Excitement, curiosity, and inspiration are emotional indicators of alignment. If an idea sparks joy or enthusiasm, it's likely an inspired action.

Why Inspired Action Is Crucial for Manifestation
Manifestation is a co-creative process. While the universe plays its part, you must play yours by taking steps toward your goals.

1. It Creates Momentum
Every action you take sends a message to the universe that you're serious about your desires. This momentum accelerates the manifestation process.

2. It Builds Confidence
Taking action reinforces your belief in your ability to achieve your goals. With each step, you become more empowered and aligned with your vision.

3. It Opens Doors
Inspired action often leads to opportunities, resources, and connections you couldn't have predicted.

Overcoming Resistance to Action
Resistance often shows up as fear, doubt, or procrastination. Here's how to overcome it and step into your power.

1. Address Fear of Failure
Fear of failure can paralyze you, but it's important to remember that every step, even missteps, brings you closer to your goal.
Action Step: Reframe failure as feedback. Ask yourself, "What can I learn from this experience?"

2. Break Down Big Goals
Feeling overwhelmed can make it hard to take action. Simplify your goals into smaller, manageable steps to build momentum.
Example: If you're manifesting a successful business, start with one action, like creating a logo or writing a mission statement.

3. Align with Your Why
Reconnect with the reason behind your desire. When you're deeply connected to your "why," it becomes easier to take inspired action.

Practical Steps to Take Inspired Action
1. Set Clear Intentions
Before taking action, clarify what you want to achieve and why. It will help ensure your actions align with your goals.
Example: If your goal is to improve your health, set an intention like, "I want to feel energized and strong every day."

2. Follow the Path of Least Resistance
Inspired actions often feel easy and natural. Pay attention to opportunities that flow effortlessly into your life.
Example: If you're manifesting a creative project, follow the ideas that come to you effortlessly rather than forcing yourself to stick to a rigid plan.

3. Take Immediate Action

When inspiration strikes, act quickly. Hesitation creates doubt and weakens the energy of your desire.

Example: If you feel inspired to attend a networking event, register immediately instead of overthinking it.

4. Celebrate Small Wins

Acknowledging progress reinforces your belief and keeps you motivated. Each step, no matter how small, is a victory.

Real-Life Stories of Inspired Action

The $500 Manifestation
In 2006, I chanted for $500 to pay bills. After the meeting, I visited a friend's house. A family member asked me to drive them to the store, and although I hesitated, I agreed. When they returned, they handed me $500 in cash, saying, "I'm sure you have some bills to pay, handle your business." A perfect example of inspired action. Saying yes to a seemingly mundane request led to the exact outcome I desired.

The New Car Journey
When manifesting my car, I felt inspired to test drive a Honda Civic, even though I didn't have the funds to buy it. The experience of driving the vehicle solidified my belief that it was mine. Weeks later, I drove home in my new Honda, proving that taking inspired action aligns you with your desires.

The Ripple Effect of Inspired Action

When you take inspired action, you don't just move closer to your goals; you inspire others to do the same. Your courage and commitment create a ripple effect, uplifting those around you and encouraging them to pursue their dreams. As we've explored, taking inspired action is a critical part of the manifestation process. It's the way you demonstrate your commitment to your desires and align your energy with your goals. But what happens when the path isn't clear or when your efforts don't seem to yield immediate results? Now is where alignment and trust in the universe come into play.

Manifestation isn't just about doing, it's about being. While inspired action creates momentum, it's equally important to trust the process, let go of control, and allow the universe to do its part. This is one of the most potent ways to Manifest Like a G.E.E., by showing up boldly and then surrendering with faith.

In the next chapter, we're not just talking about alignment, we're embodying it. It's time to lean all the way in and trust that the universe has your back. It is your invitation to stop second-guessing, let go of your resistance, and walk boldly toward your desires. You didn't come this far to play it safe. You came to manifest like a G.E.E.

So let's take everything you've been feeling, envisioning, and aligning with and put it into motion. Because now, it's go time. The universe is waiting on you.

Let's move with intention, act on divine nudges, and co-create miracles.

Chapter 12: Manifesting Through Action

Manifestation often gets misunderstood as a passive process, just visualizing and waiting for your desires to appear. While visualization and belief are critical components, it's in action that the magic truly happens. Manifestation isn't about sitting still; it's about taking intentional, inspired steps that align with your vision. The universe meets you halfway when you take action, showing you opportunities and opening doors that might otherwise remain closed.

This chapter is a guide to understanding how aligned action works within the manifestation process, why it's essential, and how you can recognize and act on the inspired nudges the universe sends your way.

The Balance Between Intention and Action

Manifestation is a dance between intention and action. Your thoughts, feelings, and visualizations set the stage, but your actions move the plot forward. Without action, even the clearest intentions can remain unrealized.

Here's how the process works:

1. Set the Intention: Get clear about what you want and focus on it with gratitude and certainty.
2. Align Your Energy: Elevate your vibration through belief, visualization, and positive emotion.
3. Take Inspired Action: Pay attention to intuitive nudges and act on them with confidence.

Inspired action is distinct from forced action. It feels natural and aligned, as though the next step reveals itself to you at the perfect time. This type of action doesn't require overthinking or second-guessing; it feels right in the moment, even if it requires courage or stepping out of your comfort zone.

Imagine a car at the top of a hill. Setting the intention is like starting the engine, and aligning your energy is like steering in the right direction. But it's the action of releasing the brake that allows the car to move forward. Without releasing the brake, without action, you remain stuck in place, no matter how much gas you give the engine.

The Power of Saying Yes to Opportunities
Often, the path to your desires isn't linear. The universe may present opportunities that seem unrelated or unexpected. Saying "yes" to these opportunities, even when they feel outside your comfort zone, can lead you directly to what you've been manifesting.

Consider this: Imagine you've been manifesting financial abundance, and a friend invites you to a networking event. It might seem unrelated to your goal, but saying "yes" could connect you with someone offering a lucrative business opportunity.

Taking action doesn't mean you have to know every step of the journey. It's about being open and willing to move forward, even when you can't see the entire staircase. Trust that each step you take is bringing you closer to your goal.

Saying Yes in Practice
- Be Open: Pay attention to invitations, ideas, or sudden urges that align with your desires.

- Trust the Process: Understand that the universe often works in mysterious ways.
- Take Small Steps: You don't have to make giant leaps; even small actions signal your readiness to receive.

How to Recognize Inspired Action
Inspired action isn't always loud or dramatic. It often comes as a whisper or a subtle nudge. Here's how to recognize it:
1. **It Feels Exciting or Right:** Inspired actions often carry a sense of excitement or alignment, even if they require courage.
2. **It's Persistent:** If an idea or thought keeps returning to you, it's likely an inspired nudge.
3. **It Happens Naturally:** You may find yourself in the right place at the right time or discover opportunities effortlessly.
4. **It's Immediate:** Sometimes, you feel a sudden urge to act, like sending an email, making a phone call, or looking something up.

When these moments arise, trust them. The faster you act on inspiration, the more momentum you create in your manifestation process.

Overcoming Fear of Action
Taking action can feel daunting, especially if it pushes you outside your comfort zone. Fear is normal, but it's essential to recognize that growth and manifestations often require stepping into the unknown.

Fear often disguises itself as practicality or hesitation. You might find yourself thinking, "What if it doesn't work?" or "What if I fail?" But these thoughts are just resistance to the change you've been asking for.

Practical Strategies to Overcome Fear:
1. **Focus on the End Result:** Remind yourself why you're taking the action. Visualize the outcome to motivate you.
2. **Break It Down:** Start with small, manageable steps to build confidence.
3. **Reframe Fear as Excitement:** Fear and excitement feel similar in the body. Shift your perspective to see fear as a sign you're on the brink of growth.
4. **Trust Yourself:** Remember that the universe supports those who take action. Trust that it will guide every step of the way.

Personal Story: Manifesting First Class Travel

A couple of years ago, I decided to fly only first class. A bold declaration because, at that point, I had never flown first class in my life. But I wanted the experience, and I believed I was worthy of it.

I started visualizing the experience in vivid detail. I saw myself walking confidently into the airport and hearing the announcement: "Now boarding first class." I imagined stepping onto the plane, turning left instead of right, and settling into the spacious first-class seat. I pictured myself enjoying the legroom, the complimentary cocktails, and the attentive service. I consistently asked myself, "Why do I only fly first class?" and "Why do I always board with zone 1?"

I had fun imagining myself in different outfits and seeing different passengers, gate agents, and flight attendants each time I visualized my first-class experience. I had zero concerns about how this would happen, and I trusted the process.

About two weeks later, I needed to make travel arrangements to Florida. I woke up one morning at 6 a.m. with an unshakable urge to search for plane tickets. Within minutes, I found a round-trip, first-class, Delta Airlines ticket for $218, a price I couldn't believe. I booked it immediately, feeling the rush of alignment and gratitude.

On the day of the flight, the airport is packed. Lines stretched for what felt like miles, and panic started to creep in. I worried about missing my flight, as I noticed the TSA line ended at the food court. As I wandered through the chaos, I thought to myself, "Where in the hell am I supposed to go," and on cue, I heard someone yell, "First class, go that way!" I asked for directions, and before I knew it, an airport employee was personally escorting me past hundreds of people standing on the other side of the ropes. I breezed through security and reached my gate within 15 minutes of arriving at the Hartsfield-Jackson Airport in Atlanta on a Friday morning, which is unheard of.

Sitting in my first-class seat felt surreal. I sipped my cocktail, stretched my legs, while the coach passengers trudged on board and found their way to their average-sized seats. I smiled, knowing without a doubt I had manifested this experience.

This story taught me two things:
1. Manifestation works when you align your energy with your desires and take inspired action.
2. The universe rewards clarity, trust, and belief.

Practical Steps for Manifesting Through Action

1. Set a Clear Intention: Be specific about what you want. Write it down, visualize it, and focus on it with gratitude.
2. Stay Open to Opportunities: Look for signs, ideas, and nudges that align with your intention.
3. Act Quickly: When inspiration strikes, don't hesitate. Take the

first step, even if it's small.
4. **Trust the Process:** Release attachment to the outcome and trust that every action is leading you closer to your goal.
5. **Evaluate Progress:** Reflect on how your actions are bringing you closer to your desires and adjust as needed.

The Ripple Effect of Action

Every action you take sends ripples through the universe. By aligning your actions with your desires, you create momentum that attracts more opportunities, resources, and synchronicities. Think of manifestation as planting a garden. Visualization is sowing the seeds, belief is watering them, and action is tending to them. With consistent care, your garden will bloom in ways that exceed your imagination.

In Manifesting Through Action, we explored the importance of aligning your thoughts, emotions, and actions to bring your desires to life. Taking inspired steps toward your goals creates powerful momentum, signaling to the universe that you're ready to receive.

But manifestation isn't just about the actions you take; it's also about the energy you project. One of the most effective ways to align your energy is through visualization. By creating a vivid mental picture of your desired reality, you activate your imagination, elevate your vibration, and connect deeply with the emotions of already having what you want.

In the next chapter, Visualization Mastery, we'll dive into advanced techniques to harness the power of your imagination and make visualization an even more impactful part of your manifestation practice.

Chapter 13: Visualization Mastery

Visualization is one of the most powerful tools in the manifestation toolkit. It's the act of intentionally creating mental images of your desired outcome, aligning your mind and emotions with the reality you want to attract. While many people have heard of visualization, few truly understand how to maximize its potential. This chapter will transform the way you approach visualization, turning it into a practice that not only excites your imagination but also rewires your brain and elevates your vibration.

Muhammad Ali said, "I am the greatest. I said that even before I knew I was." He didn't wait to become the champion; he saw it in his mind first and believed it to be true. That's the power of imagination. He visualized it, embodied it, and the world responded.

When done correctly, visualization allows you to embody your future self and live your desired reality before it physically manifests. This mastery of the mind's eye amplifies the three dimensions of manifestation, gratitude, emotion, and elevation, making the process magnetic.

Why Visualization Works
1. **Engaging the Brain's Reticular Activating System (RAS)**
Visualization programs the RAS to focus on opportunities that align with your desires. When you repeatedly visualize your goal, the RAS filters out distractions and guides your awareness to people, places, and experiences that support your vision.
2. **Triggering Neural Pathways through Mental Rehearsal.** The brain doesn't distinguish between a vividly imagined scenario and reality. When you visualize with intense emotion, you activate the same neural pathways as you would if you

were physically experiencing the event. This process strengthens your belief in the possibility, aligning your thoughts and actions with your goal.

3. **Elevating Vibrations through Emotional Connection**
Visualization isn't just about seeing, it's about feeling. By infusing your visualization practice with gratitude, joy, and excitement, you align your energy with the frequency of your desire, making it easier for the universe to deliver.

Mastering the Art of Visualization

Step 1: Set the Stage
Create a quiet, distraction-free space where you can fully immerse yourself. Sit or lie down in a comfortable position, close your eyes, and take a few deep breaths to center your mind.

Step 2: Engage All Your Senses
Vivid visualization goes beyond seeing; it's about engaging all your senses. Imagine:
- What does your desire look like?
- What does it sound like?
- How does it feel emotionally and physically?
- Are there any specific scents or tastes involved?

Example: If you're visualizing your dream home, imagine running your hand along the kitchen countertop, hearing laughter echo through the rooms, smelling fresh flowers on the dining table, and feeling the warmth of sunlight streaming through the windows.

Step 3: Incorporate Gratitude

Begin and end your visualization practice with gratitude. Imagine yourself saying, "Thank you for this incredible reality," as though your desire has already manifested, which amplifies the emotional charge of your practice.

Step 4: Make It a Daily Practice

Consistency is key. Even five minutes a day of focused visualization can make a significant impact over time. Pair this practice with affirmations to reinforce your belief in the outcome.

Common Pitfalls and How to Avoid Them

Lack of Emotional Engagement

Simply "seeing" the outcome isn't enough. To amplify the power of visualization, connect deeply with the emotions your desire brings.
Solution: Focus on how you'll feel once your goal manifests, joy, peace, excitement, and let those emotions flood your body.

Focusing on the 'How' Instead of the 'What'

Obsessing over how your desire will come to fruition creates resistance. Trust that the universe will handle the details.
Solution: Visualize the result and allow the steps to unfold naturally.

Inconsistency in Practice

Sporadic visualization sends mixed signals to the universe.
Solution: Commit to making visualization a part of your daily routine, even if it's just for a few minutes.

Advanced Techniques for Visualization Mastery

Visualization Journaling

Write down vivid descriptions of your desired reality as though it's already happened. Use the present tense and rich detail to engage your imagination.

Vision Movies

Create a digital vision board or slideshow with images and music that represent your goals. Watch it regularly to reinforce your vision.

Guided Visualization Meditations

Use guided meditations to take your visualization practice to the next level. These can help you stay focused and immerse yourself in the experience.

Manifestation Story Highlight: The Power of Visualization

During my car manifestation journey, visualization was a pivotal practice. I didn't just imagine driving the black Accord; I recorded a video of myself test-driving a car, watched it repeatedly, and felt the excitement of ownership every time. I even filled out a pretend title application and bill of sale as if I already owned the car. These actions didn't just keep my focus sharp; they aligned my energy with the reality I wanted to create. Visualization allowed me to stay connected to my goal, even when external circumstances seemed uncertain.

Embodying Your Future Self

It's about more than imagining. Visualization mastery is about embodying the energy of your future self, feeling gratitude for what's coming, and trusting the process. When you engage your mind, heart, and senses in this practice, you accelerate the manifestation of your desires.

Visualization is one of the most powerful tools in your manifestation toolkit, allowing you to align your thoughts, emotions, and energy with the reality you wish to create. By mastering the art of visualization, you've learned how to embody your desires and amplify the manifestation process.

But even with strong visualization practices and alignment, challenges can still arise. Life's unexpected twists and turns might test your focus and commitment, making it essential to stay resilient and maintain your vibration. In the next section, Navigating Challenges, we'll dive into strategies for identifying and overcoming blocks, surrendering control, and staying aligned during setbacks. These lessons will empower you to manifest with clarity and confidence, no matter what comes your way.

Part 4: Navigating Challenges

Chapter 14: Manifestation Blocks

Manifesting Like A G.E.E. is a journey of aligning your energy, thoughts, and actions to bring your desires to life. But what happens when, despite your best efforts, things don't seem to flow? Often, the culprit lies in hidden blocks that create resistance and prevent your manifestations from materializing. These blocks can be subtle, sneaking in as self-doubt, fear, or deeply rooted limiting beliefs.

Before diving into how to overcome these blocks, it's essential to acknowledge their presence as a natural part of the process. Everyone faces resistance at some point; it's not a failure but an opportunity for growth and alignment.

Limiting Beliefs
Limiting beliefs are subconscious thoughts that shape how you see the world and yourself. They might sound like:
- "I'm not good enough to achieve my goal."
- "People like me have to work hard for money."
- "I don't deserve love and happiness."

These beliefs act like invisible walls, keeping your desires at bay because they contradict the vibrational frequency of what you want to manifest.

Example Reminder: Remember the story I shared about meditating for an hour to manifest $500? While the universe delivered the money, a limiting belief about scarcity led to a misuse of those funds, delaying future manifestations. This example highlights how unchecked beliefs can derail even the most potent results.

Fear of Change
Even when we consciously want something, fear of the unknown can create resistance. The mind craves comfort, and change, no matter how positive, can trigger subconscious concerns like:
 - "What if this doesn't work out?"
 - "What if I'm not ready for this responsibility?"

Negative Patterns or Habits
Repeated behaviors or thought patterns, such as procrastination, pessimism, or toxic self-talk, can slow down or block the manifestation process. The energy you put out daily shapes your reality, so consistent negativity can repel your desires.

Attachment to the Outcome
Holding on too tightly to how or when something will happen creates resistance. This attachment signals to the universe that you don't trust the process, which disrupts the flow of abundance.

Overcoming Manifestation Blocks

Rewriting Limiting Beliefs

Start by identifying the limiting beliefs holding you back.
Write them down and challenge their validity:
 - Replace "I'm not good enough" with "I am worthy of all the abundance the universe has to offer."
 - Replace "Money is hard to come by" with "Money flows to me effortlessly and consistently."

Embracing Fear as a Catalyst for Growth
Instead of avoiding fear, view it as a sign that you're stepping into uncharted territory. Practice self-compassion and remind yourself that growth always involves some discomfort.

Personal Story Reminder: When my car broke down during my manifestation journey, it could have been paralyzing. Instead, I used that challenge as fuel to keep visualizing, taking inspired action, and trusting the process. It was a pivotal moment that reminded me to focus on possibilities rather than obstacles.

Awareness is the first step. Keep a journal to track recurring thoughts and behaviors, then actively choose to replace them. For example:
  - Swap "I'll never finish this" with "I'm making steady progress."
  - Replace endless scrolling on social media with a 10-minute visualization practice.

Detaching from the How and When
We'll dive deeper into detachment in the next chapter on surrender, but for now, it's enough to remember that detachment doesn't mean giving up. Instead, it's about trusting the process and knowing that your desires will manifest at the perfect time.

Practical Exercises for Clearing Blocks
1. The Inner Dialogue Check-In
Set a timer for five minutes and write down all the thoughts you've had about a particular manifestation. Are they empowering or limiting? Use this clarity to rewrite negative narratives.

2. The Gratitude Flip
Whenever you feel frustrated or stuck, write down three things you're grateful for in that moment. Gratitude instantly shifts your energy, making it easier to let go of resistance.

3. Visualization with Reassurance
Visualize your desire, but instead of obsessing over details, focus on the feeling of already having it. End your visualization

with the affirmation: "This or something better is already aligning for me."

Manifestation Story Highlight: The Car Manifestation Journey

Let's revisit my journey of manifesting a car in under 30 days. One major block I faced was the fear of not having the $2,500 down payment, especially after learning I hadn't won the contest I entered. It would have been easy to let this block stop me, but instead, I chose to lean into trust and take inspired actions like meditating, visualizing, and scripting.

When I overcame my fear and took consistent action, the universe provided unexpected solutions, like a friend helping me secure a 401k loan and the dealership accepting a post-dated check. This story is a powerful reminder that blocks are overcome when you stay aligned, persistent, and open to possibilities.

From Blocks to Breakthroughs

Manifestation blocks are not the end of the road; they're stepping stones to greater alignment. When you acknowledge and clear these obstacles, you open the door to infinite possibilities. Remember, every block you face is an invitation to grow, align, and step into your highest self.

In the next chapter, The Power of Surrender, we'll explore how to release attachment and fully trust the manifestation process, allowing the universe to deliver in miraculous ways.

Chapter 15: The Power of Surrender

In the manifestation process, surrender is one of the most challenging yet essential steps. It requires letting go of attachment to the outcome and trusting that the universe is working on your behalf. While it's natural to want to control when and how your desires come to fruition, true manifestation happens when you let go, create space for miracles, and prepare to receive.

Surrender is not about giving up; it's about releasing resistance. It's the act of declaring your desires with certainty, taking inspired action, and then stepping back to trust the process. In this chapter, we'll explore why surrender matters, the delicate balance between intention and letting go, and practical steps to incorporate surrender into your manifestation practice.

Why Surrender Matters in Manifestation
Surrender aligns your energy with trust and faith. When you hold on too tightly to your desires, you inadvertently create resistance, signaling doubt to the universe. This resistance blocks the flow of abundance and delays the manifestation process.

Imagine the universe as a trusted friend who has promised to bring you a special gift. If you call, text, and pester them every five minutes asking when they'll deliver it, it shows a lack of trust in their word. The same applies to the universe; constant worry and obsession send the message that you don't believe your desires are already on their way.

Surrender is about having faith that what you've asked for is already yours, even if you can't see it yet. It's about staying aligned with gratitude and trust, knowing that the universe works in perfect timing.

When you surrender:
- You allow the universe to work in ways you may not have anticipated.
- You release the heavy energy of worry and doubt, creating space for your desires to flow.
- You align yourself with the natural rhythm of manifestation, which often brings results faster than expected.

The Balance Between Intention and Surrender
One of the most critical aspects of surrender is balancing your intention with trust. Think of it as setting the GPS for your destination and then trusting the route rather than trying to control every turn.

1. Set Clear Intentions
Manifestation begins with clarity. Get specific about what you want and why it matters. Use visualization, affirmations, and gratitude to align your energy with your desires.

2. Release the How
The 'how' is not your responsibility. Trust that the universe knows the best way to bring your desires to fruition. Avoid overthinking or trying to manipulate the outcome; it creates unnecessary resistance.

3. Prepare to Receive
Align your actions and mindset with the belief that your desires are already on their way. Take inspired action when opportunities arise, but remain detached from the outcome.

Surrendering is not about passivity; it's about trusting the process while staying aligned and open to receiving in ways you may not have anticipated.

How to Practice Surrender

1. Release Attachment to the Outcome

Attachment creates resistance. When you focus too much on when or how your desires will manifest, you block their flow. Trust that the universe is orchestrating everything in your favor, even if it doesn't look exactly as you imagined.

2. Focus on Gratitude

Gratitude is one of the fastest ways to shift your energy. By appreciating what you already have, you align yourself with abundance and send a powerful message of trust to the universe. Gratitude also reinforces your faith that everything is unfolding perfectly.

3. Let Go of Fear and Doubt

Fear and doubt are natural emotions, but they create energetic blocks. When you notice these feelings creeping in, counter them with affirmations, journaling, or a gratitude practice.

4. Stay Present

Surrender requires staying rooted in the present moment. Avoid fixating on the future or worrying about past failures. The present is where your power lies.

Personal Story: Manifesting $50,000 by Letting Go

A couple of years ago, I decided to set a bold intention: "I'm so happy and grateful now that I have $50,000 of unexpected income." I had no idea where this money would come from, but I was committed to manifesting it.

I started by visualizing the money in my bank account every day. I found screenshots of account balances that showed that amount and saved them on my phone. Each morning, I spent time feeling grateful as though the money was already mine. I wrote down my intention in my gratitude journal, affirming my gratitude for this unexpected windfall.

I set a 30-day deadline and placed sticky notes around my workstation to remind myself to be grateful. These notes served as constant reinforcement of my belief and helped me stay aligned with my intention.

While I took these actions, I consciously let go of the how. I didn't obsess over where the money would come from. I allowed myself to enjoy the process, treating it like a game. About 21 days into the process, I received an email from the government. The subject line read: Your Student Loan Debt Forgiveness Application Has Been Approved.

I was stunned because I hadn't applied for forgiveness. The email went on to explain that $25,000 of my student loan debt was forgiven because I had held the loans for a long time. The message ended with, "No further action is required on your part."

I was in awe. To complete the manifestation, about one year later, the remaining $25,000 of my student loan debt was forgiven because the school I graduated from had some shady practices and had shut down all of its campuses. I also got two refund checks for the amounts that I paid towards the loans. While I hadn't received $50,000 in cash, and it took longer than 30 days, this unexpected debt forgiveness was a direct manifestation of my intention. It was a clear demonstration of how surrender works. I set the intention, took inspired action, and allowed the universe to bring my desire in its own way.

As Gabrielle Bernstein, bestselling author and spiritual teacher known for 'The Universe Has Your Back', says, "When you think you've surrendered, surrender more."

Her words are a powerful reminder that proper alignment isn't a one-time decision; it's a continual practice of letting go and leaning into trust, again and again.

The $50,000 taught me the power of letting go and trusting that the universe always has my back. It was another reminder that when I align, trust, and release control, I Manifest Like a G.E.E.

The Role of Faith in Surrender
Faith is the cornerstone of surrender. It's the belief that the universe is always conspiring in your favor, even when you can't see the evidence. Faith allows you to let go of fear and trust that everything is working out perfectly.

Building Faith Through Practice

- Reflect on past manifestations where things worked out unexpectedly.
- Use affirmations like, "I trust the universe to provide for me abundantly."
- Surround yourself with people, books, and resources that reinforce your trust in the process.

Practical Tools for Surrender

1. Visualization and Gratitude Journaling
Spend a few minutes each day visualizing your desires as already fulfilled. Follow this with a gratitude journaling practice to reinforce your faith and alignment.

2. Meditation for Letting Go
Practice meditations focused on surrender. Imagine releasing your desires into the universe's hands and feeling at peace, knowing they are being taken care of.

3. Affirmations to Reinforce Trust
Repeat affirmations daily, such as:
- "I let go of all resistance and trust the process."
- "I am open to receiving abundance in all forms."

4. Inspired Action
Take actions that align with your belief in your manifestation, but remain detached from the outcome, showing the universe that you are ready to receive.

Lessons from Surrender
Surrender is a practice of trust, faith, and alignment. It's about letting go of the need to control and allowing the universe to work its magic.

When you let go:
- You create space for unexpected opportunities and miracles.
- You align yourself with the natural flow of abundance.
- You experience greater peace and joy, knowing that everything is working out perfectly.

Letting go and surrendering to the process is one of the most profound acts of trust in manifestation. When you release your grip on the outcome, you create space for the universe to work its magic in ways you could never anticipate. But surrendering doesn't mean challenges won't arise; it means you've equipped yourself to face them with grace and resilience.

As you deepen your practice, you may encounter moments of doubt, delays, or external obstacles that test your faith. These challenges are not roadblocks but opportunities to grow, align, and clarify your desires. In the next chapter, Manifesting Through Challenges, we'll explore how to navigate these moments and stay in alignment, no matter what life throws your way.

Chapter 16: Manifesting Through Challenges

Manifestation often feels effortless when life flows smoothly. But what about when things don't go as planned? When setbacks, delays, or doubts arise, it can feel like the universe is working against you. These moments are not signs to give up but opportunities to strengthen your alignment and deepen your trust.

Challenges are not here to block you; they're here to teach, refine, and prepare you. This chapter explores strategies to stay aligned during tough times, turning obstacles into stepping stones, and keeping your energy focused on your desired outcome.

Why Challenges Arise During Manifestation

Testing Your Commitment
- Challenges often arise to test your faith and commitment to your desires. The universe may ask, "Do you truly believe this is possible? Are you ready to step into this version of yourself?"
- These tests are invitations to double down on your belief and maintain unwavering focus, even in the face of uncertainty.

Example Reminder: During my car manifestation journey, when I discovered I hadn't won the contest I had pinned my hopes on, it could have crushed my motivation. Instead, I chose to trust that the car was already mine in the energetic realm, regardless of external circumstances.

Clearing Resistance
Sometimes challenges reveal subconscious blocks, such as limiting beliefs or fears, that you need to address before your desire can manifest.
For example, if financial struggles arise while manifesting abundance, it may indicate a lingering belief in scarcity that needs to be cleared.

Preparing You for the Bigger Picture
Delays or roadblocks often mean the universe is orchestrating events for your highest good. What feels like a setback is a setup for something better than you imagined.

Staying Aligned During Difficult Times
1. **Revisit Your Why**
    - When challenges arise, reconnect with the reason you're manifesting your desire. Ask yourself:
        - Why do I want this?
        - How will it improve my life?
    - Your "why" serves as your anchor, keeping you grounded in your vision and purpose.
2. **Lean on Gratitude**
    - Gratitude is one of the quickest ways to raise your vibration during challenging times. It shifts your focus from what's going wrong to what's going right, making space for solutions to flow.
    - Exercise: Start a "Gratitude in Hard Times" journal. For every perceived setback, write down three things you're grateful for that the challenge has revealed, such as lessons, insights, or hidden strengths.
3. **Embrace Detachment**
    - Detachment is not about giving up; it's about trusting the process and releasing the need to control when or how your desire manifests. Challenges often force you to let

go of the "how" and lean into trust.
- Affirmation: "I trust that everything is unfolding perfectly for my highest good."

4. **Visualize Beyond the Challenge**
   - When obstacles arise, it's tempting to focus on the problem. Instead, use visualization to keep your energy aligned with the outcome you want. Imagine yourself already living the reality you're manifesting, despite current circumstances.
   - Example Reminder: When my car broke down, I visualized myself driving the black Accord with complete confidence, even though I didn't know how I'd secure the down payment. This practice kept my energy focused on the result rather than the temporary challenge.

Practical Tools for Navigating Challenges

Pause and Reflect
- Take a step back and ask yourself:
  - What is this situation teaching me?
  - Is there a hidden opportunity or lesson here?
- Journaling is a powerful tool for processing your emotions and uncovering insights.

Energy Reset Practices
- Challenges often disrupt your energy. Use these practices to reset and realign:
  - *Meditation*: Quiet your mind and reconnect with your vision.
  - Movement: Activities like yoga or walking can help release stagnant energy.
  - Breathwork: Deep, intentional breathing calms the nervous system and restores balance.

Affirmation Rituals
- Repeat affirmations to remind yourself of your power and the

universe's support:
- "I am divinely guided and supported in all that I do."
- "Every challenge I face brings me closer to my desires."

Celebrate Small Wins
- Acknowledge every bit of progress, no matter how small. Celebrating your wins reinforces the belief that you're moving forward, even when the path feels slow.

Manifestation Story Highlight: Triumphing Over Challenges

During the $500 manifestation, I meditated with complete trust, and within an hour, the money appeared from an unexpected source. However, using the funds for a scam investment instead of paying my bills was a misaligned action, which delayed future manifestations. This experience taught me that staying aligned in belief and in action is crucial for sustainable results. Challenges are here to teach us, not stop us.

Transforming Obstacles into Opportunities
1. **Reframe the Narrative**
   - Instead of viewing challenges as roadblocks, see them as stepping stones. Ask yourself:
     - How can I use this situation to grow?
     - What is the universe trying to show me?
2. **Strengthen Your Trust Muscle**
   - Every challenge you overcome strengthens your ability to trust the process. Trust isn't just a feeling; it's a practice of resilience and surrender.

As we've explored, challenges shouldn't deter you but should strengthen your alignment and commitment. They're a reminder that even in difficult moments, you have the power to choose gratitude, trust, and resilience. By embracing these lessons, you transform obstacles into opportunities and align more deeply with the flow of the universe.

Now that you've learned how to navigate challenges and stay aligned, it's time to take manifestation to the next level. In this final part of the book, we'll expand on how manifestation principles apply to all areas of life, from health and well-being to living as the highest version of yourself. By integrating these practices into every facet of your existence, you'll create a life that's not only abundant but holistically fulfilling.

Let's dive into how you can bring these teachings to life in the areas that matter most.

Part 5: Expanding Manifestation to All Areas of Life

Chapter 17: Health and Well-Being

Health and well-being are the foundation of a fulfilling life. Without vitality and balance, it's challenging to fully embrace opportunities, achieve goals, and find joy in everyday life. Yet, maintaining optimal health extends far beyond physical habits like eating well and exercising; it begins with the mind.

Your thoughts, emotions, and beliefs shape your body's reality. When you align your mindset with the frequency of wellness and abundance, you activate the body's natural ability to heal, restore, and thrive.

In this chapter, we'll dive deep into the mind-body connection, explore the transformative power of gratitude and visualization in promoting health, and provide actionable tools to support your journey to well-being.

The Mind-Body Connection

The connection between your mind and body is undeniable. Science and spirituality both affirm that your thoughts and emotions directly impact your physical health.

For example, positive thoughts and emotions, such as joy, gratitude, and love, stimulate the release of feel-good chemicals like serotonin, dopamine, and oxytocin. These chemicals strengthen your immune system, reduce inflammation, and promote overall well-being.

On the other hand, negative emotions like stress, fear, and anger trigger the release of cortisol and adrenaline. While these hormones are helpful in short bursts (such as during emergencies), prolonged exposure can weaken your immune system, disrupt sleep, and lead to chronic illnesses.

Louise Hay taught that every physical ailment has an emotional root, and that healing begins when we shift our thoughts and offer our bodies love, forgiveness, and affirmation. The good news is that you can consciously choose thoughts and emotions that support your health. By cultivating practices like mindfulness, gratitude, and visualization, you align your body with the vibration of wellness.

Gratitude as a Healing Tool
Gratitude is one of the most powerful and accessible tools for enhancing health. It shifts your focus from what's wrong to what's right, raising your vibration and signaling your body to operate in a state of harmony.

Research shows that practicing gratitude:
- Reduces symptoms of depression and anxiety.
- Lowers blood pressure and improves heart health.
- Strengthens the immune system.

Gratitude also activates the brain's reward system, releasing dopamine and creating a positive feedback loop. The more grateful you feel, the healthier and happier you become.

How to Practice Gratitude for Wellness
- **Morning Gratitude Ritual:** Begin your day by listing three things you're grateful for about your body. For example, "I'm grateful for my strong legs that carry me," or "I'm thankful for my healthy lungs that allow me to breathe deeply."

- **Gratitude Meditation:** Visualize each part of your body and express silent gratitude for its function and presence.
- **Gratitude Journal:** Before bed, write about moments of well-being you experienced during the day, no matter how small.

When you consistently focus on gratitude, you shift your body into a state of healing and resilience.

The Power of Visualization in Healing

Visualization is a cornerstone of manifestation, and it's equally transformative for health. By imagining yourself as vibrantly healthy, you align your energy with the frequency of wellness, signaling your body to heal and thrive. I'm talking about seeing yourself whole, strong, glowing, and energized before the evidence ever shows up. When you close your eyes and feel the vitality in your body like it's already yours, you give your cells a new instruction manual to follow. That's not woo-woo, that's energy in motion, and your body listens.

Steps to Effective Visualization for Healing

1. **Create a Clear Image:** Imagine yourself in a scenario where you feel radiant and firm. For example, picture yourself hiking a beautiful trail, full of energy and joy.
2. **Engage All Senses:** Feel the warmth of the sun, hear the rustling leaves, smell the fresh air, and sense your body moving effortlessly.
3. **Infuse Gratitude:** As you visualize, feel deeply grateful for your health as though it's already your reality.

Here's the wild part: your brain doesn't know the difference between what's real and what you vividly imagine. That means when you visualize yourself healing, your brain fires the same signals as if it were actually happening in real time. You're literally rewiring your system for wellness. The rewiring sends messages throughout your body to release feel-good hormones, strengthen your immune system, and activate your natural ability to recover and thrive. Your imagination isn't just powerful, it's medicine.

The Energy of Healing

Everything is energy, including you. Your body is a beautifully intelligent system made up of cells, tissues, and organs that all vibrate at specific frequencies. When your energy is in harmony with health, your body knows exactly what to do. It begins to recalibrate, restore, and realign. Healing isn't just physical; it's vibrational, and when you tune into the frequency of wellness, you give your body permission to thrive.

Using Energy for Healing

One effective technique is visualizing healing light. Here's how:
- Close your eyes and take a few deep breaths.
- Imagine a ball of radiant white light above your head.
- Visualize this light descending and enveloping your entire body, repairing cells, and restoring harmony.
- Feel the warmth and comfort of the light, and repeat affirmations like:
    - "Every cell in my body vibrates with health."
    - "My body is strong, resilient, and whole."

By combining visualization with positive affirmations, you align your energy with the vibration of wellness, enhancing your body's natural healing processes.

Practical Steps for Cultivating Health and Well-Being

1. **Meditation:** Dedicate time daily to quieting your mind and connecting with your body. Even 5–10 minutes can reduce stress and support healing.
2. **High-Vibrational Foods:** Nourish your body with fresh, nutrient-dense foods that support vitality. Think colorful fruits, leafy greens, and whole grains.
3. **Mindful Movement:** Engage in activities that bring you joy, like yoga, dancing, or walking in nature. Movement boosts energy, improves mood, and enhances circulation.
4. **Affirmations for Health:** Repeat statements like "I am grateful

for my vibrant health" or "My body knows how to heal itself."
5. **Daily Gratitude:** Cultivate a habit of appreciating your body and its functions, even during illness or discomfort. Gratitude transforms your perspective and accelerates healing.

Personal Story: Healing Myself Overnight

One of the most transformative moments in my health journey happened during a work trip. I had a significant meeting scheduled out of town, which required a four-hour drive. The trip itself was smooth, and I felt fantastic the entire way.

However, as soon as I pulled into the hotel parking lot, I noticed a tickle in my throat. Within minutes, my head started to ache, and my body felt heavy and sluggish. It became clear that I was coming down with something, and the symptoms were escalating quickly.

I couldn't afford to be sick, not now. Determined to feel better by morning, I bought a packet of vitamin C powder and a bottle of water from the hotel market's limited selection of healthcare items. Once in my room, I poured the vitamin C powder into the water and gratefully drank the entire bottle before I lay down to meditate. I closed my eyes and imagined a ball of pure white light hovering above me. As I took slow, deep breaths, I visualized the light growing brighter and descending over my body. In my mind, I chanted repeatedly, "Thank you for my healing, thank you for my healing," focusing on feelings of gratitude and wellness.

The light began to feel warm, almost tangible, and it worked to repair and rejuvenate me from the inside out. I continued the meditation until I drifted off to sleep, and when I woke up the next morning, every symptom was gone. I felt completely renewed, clear-headed, energized, and deeply aligned. That moment reminded me that healing doesn't always have to take weeks or months. When you combine gratitude, visualization, and unwavering belief, you unlock a divine power within that can shift everything in an instant.

Trusting in Your Body's Wisdom

Your body is a miraculous vessel with the innate ability to heal itself. Trusting in its wisdom, aligning with the vibration of health, and practicing gratitude and visualization can unlock levels of well-being you never thought possible.

Health is not just the absence of illness; it's a state of harmony between your body, mind, and spirit. By focusing on gratitude, practicing visualization, and adopting high-vibrational habits, you can transform your health and create a life of vitality and joy.

Remember: You are a co-creator of your well-being, and the power to heal and thrive lies within you. Embrace these practices, and watch as your health flourishes in ways that feel nothing short of miraculous.

From Wellness to Action: Turning Energy into Results

A foundation of health and well-being empowers you to fully engage with the world and take the steps needed to bring your dreams to life. When your mind is clear and your body energized, you're better equipped to recognize and seize the opportunities that align with your desires.

Manifesting Like a G.E.E. takes more than just visualization and alignment. It requires movement. That means taking bold, inspired, and intentional steps that bridge the gap between the vision in your mind and the reality you're ready to live. In the next chapter, I'll show you how to transform your desires into real results through aligned action, all while staying in flow with the universe. Let's take those dreams off the vision board and bring them to life.

Chapter 18: Living Like a G.E.E.: Gratitude, Emotion, and Elevation in Action

This book has been more than just a guide to manifestation. It's been a deep dive into the mindset shifts, energetic practices, and powerful truths that unlock your ability to co-create your reality. But manifestation isn't only about attracting a new car, relationship, or career. It's about becoming. It's about evolving into the version of yourself who naturally aligns with the life you dream of living.

That's the heartbeat of my brand, Raise Your Inner G.E.E. It was born from my own journey of transformation, from the lessons I learned when I stopped surviving and started shifting. G.E.E. stands for Gratitude, Emotion, and Elevation, the three powerful forces that shape your vibration, fuel your manifestation, and reconnect you with your highest self.

My intention throughout this book has been to walk beside you, showing you not just how to understand manifestation but also how to live it. To Raise Your Inner G.E.E. means embodying gratitude as a daily habit, feeling your emotions as fuel, and elevating your energy until alignment becomes your lifestyle.

As we bring everything together in this final chapter, it's time to go beyond theory and step into embodiment. This is where you start living it fully, boldly, unapologetically. You've done the work. Now, let's unlock the version of you who is meant to rise.

The Foundations of Raising Your Inner G.E.E.

Gratitude
Throughout this book, you've seen how gratitude is the cornerstone of manifestation. It raises your vibration, shifts your focus to abundance, and creates a magnetic energy that draws in your desires.

Lesson Reminder: Gratitude is not just a practice; it's a state of being. Begin and end each day by recognizing what you're thankful for, from the smallest joys to your biggest blessings.

Emotion
Emotion is the fuel that powers your manifestations. By feeling the joy, love, and excitement of already having your desires, you align your energy with the reality you want to create.

Lesson Reminder: Use the visualization techniques you've mastered to evoke strong emotions daily, letting your heart guide you toward your highest desires.

Elevation
Elevation is about raising your vibration and expanding your consciousness. It's the moment when you step into the version of yourself that is already living your dream life.

Lesson Reminder: Practice raising your vibration through meditation, mindfulness, and actions that align with your goals. Choose thoughts, habits, and environments that keep you lifted.

Key Lessons from the Journey

The Power of Belief
Manifestation begins and ends with belief. When you genuinely

believe in your worthiness and the possibility of your desires, the universe aligns to meet you there.

Your Inner G.E.E. Practice: Strengthen your belief by affirming, visualizing, and acting as if your desires are already yours.

Trust in the Universe

Surrender and trust are essential for allowing manifestation to unfold. As we learned in The Power of Surrender, detachment doesn't mean giving up; it means letting go of control and allowing the universe to deliver in divine timing. Your Inner G.E.E. Practice: When challenges arise, remind yourself, "Everything is unfolding perfectly for my highest good."

The Role of Action

Manifestation is a co-creative process. While energy alignment is vital, taking inspired action bridges the gap between your inner vision and outer reality.

Your Inner G.E.E. Practice: Take small, consistent steps toward your goals, trusting that every action brings you closer to your desires.

The Science of Manifestation

Your mind and body are powerful allies in the manifestation process. As we learned in The Science of Manifestation, practices like visualization, gratitude, and emotional alignment are not just spiritual tools; science supports the process of reprogramming your brain and raising your vibration.

Your Inner G.E.E. Practice: Use daily visualization and gratitude practices to rewire your brain and keep your focus on abundance.

Resilience in Challenges

Challenges are not roadblocks; they are stepping stones. Every obstacle you face is an opportunity to grow, align, and clarify your desires.

Your Inner G.E.E. Practice: When faced with setbacks, pause, reflect, and realign. Use gratitude and trust to transform challenges into breakthroughs.

Becoming the Highest Version of You

Raising Your Inner G.E.E. is about embodying the energy of the person who already has everything they desire. It's about living in alignment with your most authentic self, guided by gratitude, empowered by emotion, and elevated by belief.

- Your Inner G.E.E. is Grateful: You recognize that life is abundant and filled with opportunities, even in moments of challenge.
- Your Inner G.E.E. is Emotional: You allow yourself to feel deeply, embracing joy, excitement, and love as you create your reality.

Your Inner G.E.E. is Elevated: You consistently choose to rise above limiting beliefs, negative patterns, and external doubts, stepping into your highest potential.

Manifesting Your Dream Life

The life you desire isn't some distant fantasy or far-off destination—it's a vibration, a frequency, a state of being that you can tap into right now. Every thought, every emotion, every decision you make moves you closer to that dream or keeps you stuck in patterns that no longer serve you.

When you raise your Inner G.E.E., lead with Gratitude, fuel your journey with elevated Emotion, and choose daily Elevation, you shift into alignment with the life that's already waiting for you. You don't have to chase your dreams; you attract them. You become them. Your dream life begins the moment you embody the energy of what you want, trust the timing, and walk boldly in your truth. It's not just about manifesting things; it's about becoming the version of you who naturally lives in joy, abundance, freedom, and flow.

The universe is listening. Keep your vibe high, your heart open, and your Inner G.E.E. activated. Your dream life is already unfolding.

Before we close...a couple more manifestation moments.

Even as I was finalizing the edits for this book, the Universe kept showing off.

Some manifestations take weeks. Others take a whisper. And sometimes, while you're still deciding how to phrase the next chapter, life hands you a brand-new one.

Before we close this journey together, I want to share two final manifestations that unfolded mid-manuscript, which are vivid reminders that alignment doesn't wait for perfect timing. These experiences came through while I was still writing, editing, and refining this book. Proof that when you walk in alignment, life responds in real time.

Let them serve as living, breathing evidence that the G.E.E. Framework works and that what you desire can find you even while you're in the process of becoming.

I'd like to share two final experiences that unfolded mid-manuscript, which are vivid reminders that alignment doesn't wait until the book is finished.

The Apartment on the 17th Floor

I had been visualizing myself living in a high-rise apartment. Not just any space. I imagined floor-to-ceiling windows, natural light pouring in, and a skyline view that made me feel elevated, literally and vibrationally. I practiced daily meditation and visualization for 30 days, and each time I walked into my current apartment, I closed my eyes and imagined stepping into the high-rise version instead. I mentally superimposed the vision over my reality.

Eventually, alignment led me to a beautiful complex with everything I had visualized. The property manager showed me a model unit on the 15th floor, and I fell in love with the layout and view. The approval process was easy and effortless, but I was assigned a unit on the 8th floor, which did not have nearly the view I had been visualizing. While I was grateful, I didn't feel the excitement I felt in my visualizations or while touring the model unit. The 8th floor didn't match the feeling I had been cultivating.

One night, I stumbled across a YouTube video featuring my exact floor plan in that same building, and the unit was on the 17th floor. The view was even more phenomenal than the model unit on the 15th floor. I watched the video on a loop, imagining what it would be like to wake up to that view every morning. I decided to lock in on that floor, aligning my vision with the feeling of expansion I knew was possible. I had some unexpected changes in my life, and I had to back out of the lease. I emailed the leasing office to let them know I'd be declining the unit.

About two weeks went by, and I hadn't heard anything from the leasing office to confirm that they received my email, so I called them. I was surprised to know that they had overlooked my email, but had reached out to me via phone. The nice lady on the phone said, "Oh, we left you a voicemail last week.

Unfortunately, we had to change your unit... to the 17th floor."

I didn't have to push. I didn't have to negotiate. I just had to align.

A Vacation from the Vortex
What do you know, the same energetic magic struck again.

Thursday morning, my friend texted me that she was at the airport, heading to the Dominican Republic. I smiled, shook my head, and added the DR to my list.

Later that same day, I texted a different friend, "I haven't had a vacation in a loooooong time." I had already traveled numerous times this year, but I needed sunshine. Ease. A shift.

Friday morning, a third friend replied to a post I made online. We hadn't spoken in months, but I followed the nudge to message her privately instead of replying publicly.

That private message turned into magic.

She told me she was heading to the Dominican Republic the day after Thanksgiving, which was 14 days away. I mentioned how another friend had flown there the day before, and that I was feeling called to go too.

Her response?

"Shoot, you can come with me...my roommate can't go."

She didn't know I had flight benefits through the friend who had texted me the day before. The all-inclusive resort was already covered, and all I had to do was book my flight, which cost me a whopping $148 for the round-trip.

Everything came together effortlessly. Affordable payments. Perfect timing. No chase. Just a "yes" and an open door.

From "I haven't had a vacation in a looooong time" to the invite took 17 hours. From receiving the invitation to boarding the plane, it took 14 days.

The Bigger Lesson

These weren't just manifestations. They were reminders. Proof that alignment isn't about force or perfect strategy. It's about clarity, energy, trust, and timing. You don't have to earn it through suffering. You have to become a match.

Even in the middle of editing a book about manifestation, the Universe was still responding to my vibration.

Still proving that this *work* works.

Closing Exercise: A Letter to Your Future Self

Take a sacred moment just for you. Close your eyes and visualize your highest self, the most radiant, empowered, and abundant version of who you truly are. What do they look like? How do they carry themselves? What do they believe about life, love, and possibility? Feel their energy, listen to their thoughts, and witness the confidence and clarity they move with.

Now open your journal and begin writing a heartfelt letter to that future version of you. Thank your future self for holding the vision steady, for making aligned choices, and for showing up each day with courage and consistency. Acknowledge the beauty of the life they've created; the joy, the peace, the freedom, and the abundance that flows with ease.

Use this letter to make a promise to yourself. Commit to living each day in alignment with your Inner G.E.E., guided by gratitude, fueled by emotion, and elevated by the belief that you are a powerful co-creator with the universe.

This letter is not just a reflection of who you're becoming. It is a declaration of who you are. You've done the inner work. You've raised your energy. Now, let this letter be your energetic agreement with the life you are manifesting.

Your dream life is not far away. It is already within you, waiting for you to claim it.

As we come to the end of this journey together, let me remind you of one simple truth: You are the creator of your reality. Every thought you think, every emotion you feel, and every action you take sends ripples into the universe, shaping the life you experience. Through this book, you've learned how to channel that creative power deliberately, with clarity, alignment, and intention.

The G.E.E. framework of gratitude, emotion, and elevation is more than concepts. They are the foundation for a life of purpose, joy, and abundance. Gratitude grounds you in the beauty of the present moment, unlocking a mindset of possibility. Emotion fuels your manifestations, creating a magnetic pull between you and your desires. Elevation lifts your vibration, allowing you to align with your highest self and your actual reality.

By raising your inner G.E.E., you've taken the first steps toward transforming your mindset, your energy, and your life. But this is just the beginning. Manifestation isn't a one-time event; it's a lifelong practice. With each day, you have the opportunity to deepen your alignment, refine your vision, and celebrate the miracles that unfold.

Remember, the process of manifestation isn't about perfection; it's about persistence. There will be days when doubt creeps in, challenges arise, or progress feels slow. In those moments, return to the practices in this book. Anchor yourself in gratitude. Tap into the emotions of joy and excitement for what's coming. Elevate your energy with affirmations, visualization, and inspired action. These tools are your compass, guiding you back to alignment and belief.

Your journey is uniquely yours. No one else can manifest the life you're here to create. The dreams in your heart are your soul's roadmap to greatness. Trust in them. Nurture them. And most importantly, act on them with the courage and confidence of someone who knows they are worthy.

As you step into this new chapter of your life, remember the title of this book; it's more than a name; it's a call to action. Manifest Like a G.E.E. isn't just a catchy phrase; it's a lifestyle. It's about embodying gratitude, emotion, and elevation every single day, no matter where you are on your journey.

You don't have to wait for your dreams to feel abundant or joyful. Live like it's already yours. Celebrate every step, stay aligned, and trust that the universe is always guiding you.

Dream big. Move boldly. Manifest with intention. Everything you need is already within you.

Now it's your time to shine.
With infinite gratitude and belief -

Gee

About the Author

Gelita Mimms, affectionately known as Gee, is a speaker, manifestation mentor, and the visionary behind Raise Your Inner G.E.E.. This transformational brand helps others shift their mindset and step into their highest self. G.E.E. stands for Gratitude, Emotion, and Elevation, the core principles that guide her mission and message.

With over 20 years of experience in personal development and manifestation, Gee has dedicated her life to helping people break through limiting beliefs and create a life that aligns with their deepest desires. Her journey has been one of growth, healing, and powerful transformation, and she now uses her story to inspire others to reclaim their power and manifest with intention.

Through her speaking engagements, workshops, and written work, Gee encourages others to live boldly, love fully, and trust the process of becoming. She believes that when you raise your inner G.E.E., you raise your entire life.

Learn more at RaiseYourInnerGEE.com.

www.ingramcontent.com/pod-product-compliance
Lightning Source LLC
Chambersburg PA
CBHW060610080526
44585CB00013B/767